For Bobby & Beckett

Football Type 2

First published in the UK in 2020 by Face37 Ltd
www.face37.com

Complied & edited by Rick Banks
Written by Denis Hurley

Face37 Ltd is registered in England & Wales:
3 Hodgkinsons Farm, Boot Lane, Bolton, Greater Manchester
Company № 7650982 VAT № 114509244

Typeset in F37 Neuro
www.f37foundry.com

Printed in the UK by PUSH
www.push-print.com

ISBN: 978-0-9926037-2-4

Paper by G . F Smith
GFS Max and Colorplan Lockwood Green

Preface
Denis Hurley

At the most base level, names and numbers on football shirts exist so that the watching public — in the stands and at home, looking at their televisions — can identify players.

Similarly, teams have colours so that one team can be told apart from another but, in the same way that kit design is now a big business, fonts and typefaces have grown in terms of significance, aided by the advent of squad numbering in the 1990s.

The brief for somebody sitting down to create a new football typeface can be a rather constrained one. Whereas many design missions literally start with a blank canvas, the person coming up with a new font has a series of shapes and sizes to conform to. Then, those intended for football kits must take into the account the shirts and shorts on which those shapes will appear — legibility is of course the key consideration, but the typography can't clash with the kit either.

When Football Type was published in 2013, it was as comprehensive a collation as could be of the history of the numbering and lettering that had appeared on strips. However, the time since then has seen an exponential increase in new fonts created as well as some historical tales coming to light. That is reflected in the sheer volume of this edition.

About
Denis Hurley is a freelance sports journalist based in Cork, Ireland. He runs museumof jerseys.com and squadnumbers.com

As you delve through the thread of history, patterns emerge along with the various influences from other sports as well as firms piggy-backing on the success of rivals. In later years, with the emergence of club-specific fonts, often changing year-on-year, the inspirations have tended to reflect the culture of the team, its story and surroundings.

A truly comprehensive round-up of those fonts is likely to remain elusive due to the scale of such a task. We feel, though, that this is as close to that as can be achieved. And, who knows, if the rate of progress continues, perha-ps we shall be revising it again in a few years.

1

200

442

706

1000

Right
Football Type was published in 2013. The book raised an impressive £22.5k for grassroots football club Horwich St. Mary's in Bolton.

Introduction
Rick Banks

Today, it's impossible to conceive of a football kit without a number on it — so intrinsic are the digits that they can become part of a player's brand (just think CR7). However, the first instance of numbering in a football game came in 1924, a full 61 years after the codification of the Laws of The Game.

Of course, when we say 'football', we mean the association variety — rugby union had stolen a march and the Wales-England game in Cardiff in 1922 was the first time that both teams in a Five Nations Championship game were numbered. Ireland and France followed, but, apart from a brief dalliance, Scotland held out. When King George V gently enquired of SFU (now SRU) President James Aikman Smith as to why the Scots were unnumbered, he was gruffly informed that it was a rugby match and not a cattle sale.

The need for identification, so as to aid spectators, players and officials, was growing. From the early 20th century, match programmes assigned numbers to players according to position — with participants rarely venturing away from their spot; it made it easier to tell who was who.

Transposing those numbers to shirts took longer. After a brief experiment in 1928, and again for the 1933 FA Cup final, the Football League wouldn't allow shirt numbers until the beginning of the 1939-40 season.

Left to right
Cristiano Ronaldo has his own logo, CR7, printed on his boots.

Unofficial vs official Schmeichel lettering.

Used solely as identifiers, there was little thought given to the 'design' of the numbers until the 1970s, when manufacturers began to apply their own flourishes to kits. The 1980s saw further experimentation — Umbro had a font which was outlawed due to a lack of clear visibility [p96] and the advent of squad names and numbers on shirts, first seen in the 1993 Coca-Cola Cup final, led to a commercial explosion.

As a designer, that was my first experience of typography. Obviously, when I was eight years old, I didn't know what typography was, but I remember trying to recreate 'Schmeichel' in Umbro's condensed slab serif [p112] in my school books. After pleading with my mum, she kindly bought me a replica top with the Danish super-stopper's surname printed on the back. When she gave it to me, I remember nearly crying my eyes out because the letters weren't the correct 'official' font — it was printed at a local greetings card shop. Thankfully, 25 years later, my mum understands my fanatical attention to detail.

In 1997, the Premier League released a mandatory typeface for all teams. The font was a 'stretched' version of Optima [p122]. The practice of stretching letters sends shivers down most typographers' backs — thankfully, this only happened for a relatively short period of time when desktop publishing arrived in the '90s. In 2007, a bespoke typeface replaced the 'off-the-shelf' Optima [p194] and another new font followed in 2017 [p350]. In the same year, La Liga followed suit, when they stipulated every team had to adhere to their official lettering, much to the dismay of Real Madrid [p352].

It's grown into a big business. Replica shirts bought worldwide must use official alphabets. Typically, retailers and clubs charge per letter — fine if your favourite player is Demba Ba, not so good if it's Jan Vennegoor of Hesselink [p170].

Every year, millions are spent on football shirt design. Clubs and manufacturers are ditching off-the-shelf fonts and investing in beautifully designed, custom-made typefaces to match the kit [p256] or even a whole campaign. In 2012, GBH Design designed the typeface 'Gaffer' for PUMA [p250]. This look wasn't just for shirts; it was for the entire campaign. It appeared on merchandise, footballs, boots and even featured in football video games.

In 2006, Tottenham Hotspur commissioned a branding agency to appraise their identity. Their cockerel was redrawn in a modern way and typographer Bruno Maag designed a new typeface which featured on their European shirts and consistently on all their official communications [p172]. By viewing themselves as a brand and not just a football club, Spurs became a unique market leader. 13 years later and it's still used today.

Most successful clubs have become huge brands. Manchester United has retail stores in places as far flung as Singapore. We have seen clubs wanting to increase their brand by tapping into this growing market and fan base with the exposure of pre-season tours in Asia. We have also seen clubs wanting to become more of a lifestyle brand and appeal to non-football fans. This can be seen in the Juventus rebrand [p356], and is echoed in PSG's collaboration with the Air Jordan brand [p402], integrating football into streetwear fashion.

Right
The new font for MLS launched in 2020.

Players are brands too. David Beckham raised a staggering £1 billion worldwide in shirt and boot sales in his career. This global reach is emphasized when Real Madrid, in 2012, commissioned a typographer to offer Japanese, Chinese and Arabic fans Cristiano Ronaldo shirts in their individual alphabets [p210]. Fast forward 6 years, and within 24 hours, Juventus sold half a million CR7 shirts in a day, worth a staggering £50 million – nearly half his transfer fee.

After publishing *Football Type* back in 2013, I was fortunate enough to be commissioned to design a bespoke font for the MLS [p418]. This was a dream job for me as football and typography are some of my biggest passions. At the end of the day, a well designed bespoke font helps identify a brand. It works away tirelessly and seamlessly, even when other brand assets such as colour, logo or imagery aren't around. It is a badge of distinction, a bold statement of individuality. And I can't wait to see what next season will bring.

About
Rick Banks is the founder of Face37 & F37 Foundry, an award winning graphic design studio and font foundry, servicing a global roster of clients.

1920
1960

Vesper Buick of St. Louis, Missouri, only existed for four years, taking its name due to patronage from the eponymous automobile company. The team competed in the St. Louis Soccer League, winning it twice, as well as making it to the final of the 1923-24 National Challenge Cup (now known as the US Open Cup).

Taking on Fall River Marksmen from Massachusetts, Vesper Buick lost 4-2, but they created history as they became the first documented example of a football team wearing shirt numbers.

Clubs
Fall River Marksmen &
St. Louis Vesper Buick

Typeface
Sewn

Year
1924

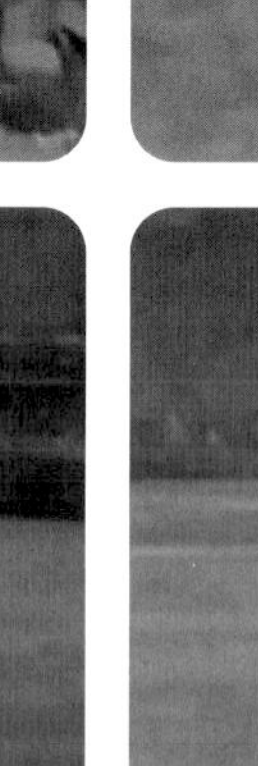

Buick

Buick

Arsenal and Chelsea created Football League history on August 25, 1928 when they took to the field for season openers, against The Wednesday and Swansea Town respectively, with shirt numbers on their backs.

The managers of the two sides, Arsenal's Herbert Chapman and Dave Calderhead of Chelsea, were good friends and it's likely they devised the plan together. However, while Chapman often took the credit, Calderhead's Chelsea had actually started the experiment in a trial game a year previously, in August 1927.

A *Press Association* article, syndicated in a number of local publications, quoted Calderhead in saying that it was done to help spectators identify players. "It certainly is helpful, particularly from the spectator's point of view," he said, "but we are not certain if it is worthwhile putting it up to the Football Association Council. Of course, we could not adopt the idea without the Football Association's permission."

The article also featured other managers' views – Tottenham Hotspur's Billy Minter and Syd King of West Ham United felt it made players look like jockeys but Chapman was in favour: "There are always a certain number of spectators who do not know the players – strangers in every sense – to whom the numbering of players would prove a great aid. For the average spectator, however, the innovation would hardly be necessary."

A year on, and the plans for numbering by Arsenal [it seems Chelsea didn't reveal their plans beforehand] received some airing in the press prior to the start of the league. On the day of the game against The Wednesday, a writer in the *Derby Daily Telegraph* took a positive view: "Much has been said about the unnecessity of this departure but, when all is said and done, there are many things to be said in its advantage.

"Spectators should value the numbering of players if only to be made cognisant with what changes the enterprising captain may make in the formation of his team dur-

EL MISMO SCORE CON QUE ESTE SE IMPUSIERA EN EL PRIMER PARTIDO

ODELL ha caído al suelo, después de devolver una pelota. Stabile, el hombre oportunista, que venía a toda marcha en dirección al arco de los visitantes frena, y sigue con la vista la trayectoria de la ball.

RODGERS, a quien el centro half Monti dejara knock-out al finalizar la brega, aparece aquí entre Tarasca y Millington, dispuesto a conjurar un momento de gran peligro para su valla.

LOS pibes de la sexta división de Huracán, que venció a Estudiantes de La Plata, en uno de los partidos preliminares del internacional jugado en el field de Boca Juniors, dando los hurras con la apostura de los cracks, frente a la tribuna oficial.

MILLINGTON, embestido por Tarascone, rechaza a duras penas. Arriba, en círculo: Kuko ha saltado sin éxito y la pelota rebota en la espalda de Stabile, bien marcado por Smith.

Club
Chelsea F.C.

Typeface
Sewn

Year
1928/29

ing the course of a game." Chelsea won 4-0 but Arsenal's numbering didn't help them as they lost 3-2. In a report on that game, the Sheffield *Daily Telegraph* made mention of the new departure: "The players had black numbers on a white background on the back of their jerseys, and doubtless the figures enable spectators, who were not familiar with the men, to identify them in the course of operations."

However, the Football League was not as keen for change to be so rapid. At a meeting on the Monday, its management committee stated they were of the opinion that: "players should not be numbered for the purpose of football matches until the question has been fully discussed and decided upon by the clubs at the next annual meeting. The committee hope that the clubs will, in the meantime, give effect to this opinion as an instruction."

Chelsea would revive the scheme for a tour of South America at the end of that 1928-29 season. So eye-catching were the numbers against the local teams that they earned the nickname 'Los Numerados'.

Club
Arsenal F.C.

Typeface
Sewn

Year
1933

Ask someone who Everton's best number 9 was and the chances are that they will answer: "Dixie Dean". They're correct — but he only wore it once.

After the Arsenal/Chelsea experiment found no traction with the Football League, shirts remained blank into the 1930s, but it was decided to trial them again for the 1933 FA Cup final between Everton and Manchester City.

Everton fielded what would become the conventional format — goalkeeper 1, full-backs 2 and 3, half-backs 4, 5 and 6 and attack 7-11, outside right to outside left. Presumably in an attempt to avoid confusion, City were numbered 12-22, but in 'reverse' — the outside-left was 12 and the goalkeeper 22. Had the numbering formats been reversed, Dean — who scored in a 3-0 win — would have been Everton's best number 14.

In the *Liverpool Echo* that evening, columnist Louis T. Kelly was in favour of numbering, but felt if it were adopted that it would be best to have both teams 1-11, not least because it would save on having two sets of shirts, 1-11 at home and 12-22 away.

Clubs

Manchester City F.C.
& Everton F.C.

Typeface
Sewn

Year
1933

Photography
James Jarche

19
17
12

Country
Sweden

Typeface
Sewn

Year
1950

Country
Uruguay

Typeface
Sewn

Year
1954

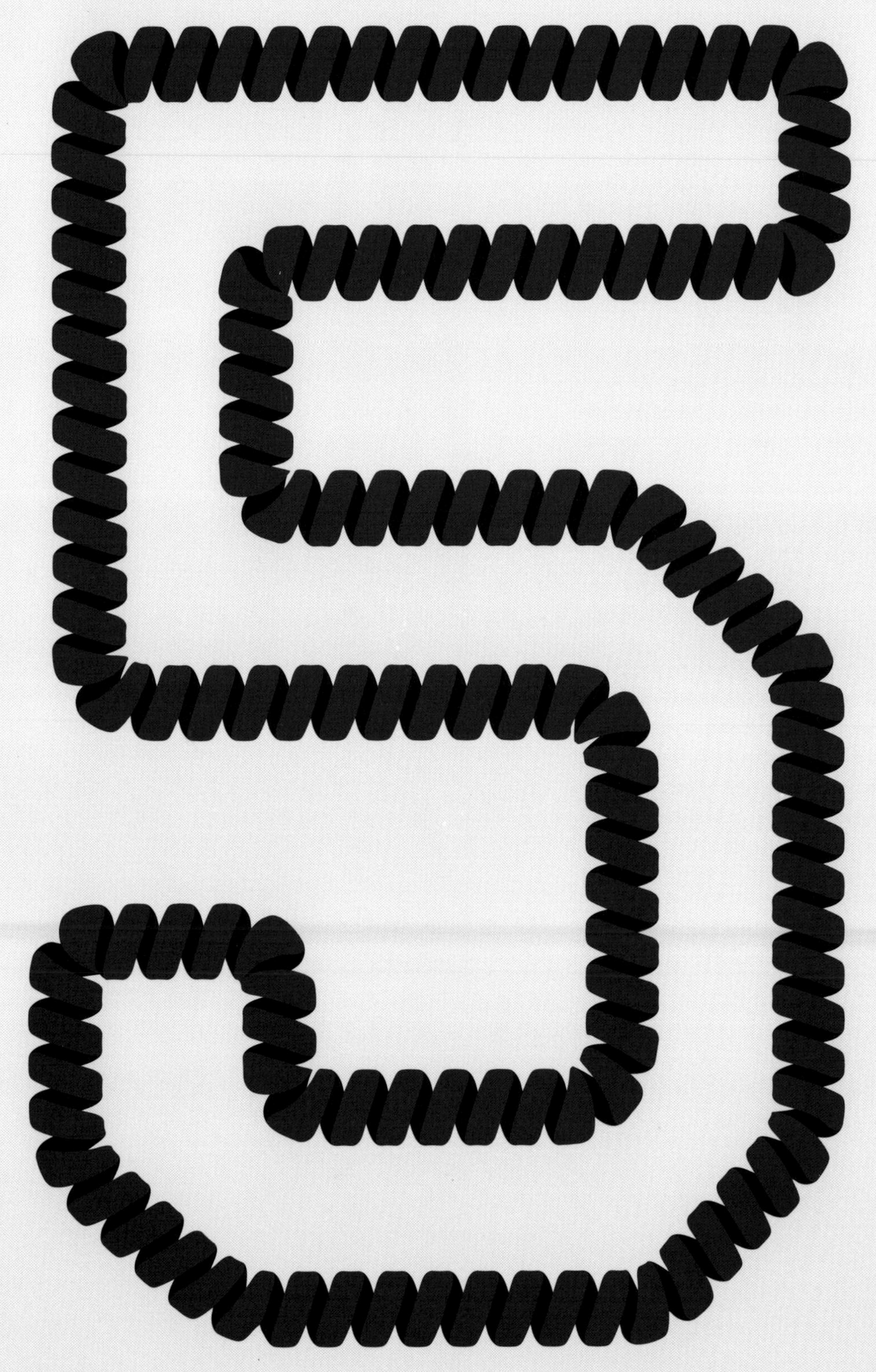

Legendary Hungarian goalkeeper-Gyula Grosics making a save during the World Cup quarter-final against Brazil at the Wankdorf Stadium, Berne, Switzerland, June 27, 1954.

Grosics, part of the 'Golden Team' which reached the World Cup final that year, had the nickname 'The Black Panther' due to his quick reflexes and his all-black kit.

During Hungary's anti-Communist revolution in 1956, Grosics took his family out of the country and looked to start a new life abroad, but he was forced to return. As his club Budapest Honved had been banned from official competition following a money-spinning world tour against FIFA's wishes, Grosics sought a transfer to glamour side Ferencvaros but instead he was sent to provincial side Tatabanya, with whom he finished his career in 1962.

The dream of representing Ferencvaros looked to have eluded him — but it was finally realised in March 2008, when the club organised a friendly against Sheffield United and invited him to keep goal.

Wearing a personalised black jersey, the 82-year-old walked to the goal one last time, controlled a back-pass and side-footed out of the box to one of his defenders. He was then replaced by 19-year-old Ádám Holczer.

After the game, Ferencvaros stated that nobody else would wear the club's No 1 shirt. The club registered the veteran for life and he appeared on every squad list the Green Eagles sent to the Hungarian FA until his death in 2014.

Country
Hungary

Typeface
Sewn

Year
1954

Country
France

Typeface
Sewn

Year
1959

1960
1970

CCCP

Before the 1966 World Cup, Umbro founder Harold Humphreys travelled to every one of the competing countries and offered them kit manufactured by his company.

According to lore, all but one of the 16 took up his offer, with the USSR mentioned as the exception. However, research by Simon Shakeshaft of the National Football Shirt Collection and Glen Isherwood of England Football Online suggests that only half of the teams wore Umbro strips.

In the picture below, Albert Shesternyov leads the Soviet team out against Turkey at Lenin Central Stadium, 1966.

While the Umbro double-diamond never joined the iconic 'CCCP' script in a first-class match, the USSR would later wear the three stripes of adidas. However, often the crest would be placed over the German firm's Trefoil.

Country
USSR

Typeface
Sewn

Year
1966

North Korea's 1966 World Cup win over Italy is regarded as one of the most incredible upsets in sport — but it's alleged that the squad didn't return home as heroes.

When the international football showcase came to England in 1966, North Korea were making history as the first Asian side to make the finals, doing so just 13 years after the end of the Korean War.

After a loss to the Soviet Union and a draw with Chile, little was expected of North Korea against Italy at Middlesbrough's Ayresome Park on July 19, 1966, but Pak Doo-ik's goal gave them victory and second place in the group.

The fairytale looked to be continuing as they raced into a 3-0 lead inside 25 minutes against Portugal at Goodison Park in the quarter-finals, but they lost 5-3. According to Korean defector Kang Chol-hwan in his book *The Aquariums of Pyongyang*, the team did not receive the homecoming they hoped for — instead they were arrested. The side was branded a disgrace and some of them were sent to the gulags after their shameful defeat.

Kang's claims have, however, been later disputed by documentarians, who claim the squad are still held in high regard by the city of Pyongyang.

1

Country
North Korea

Typeface
Sewn

Year
1966

4

Brazilian icon Pelé in the 1966 World Cup at Goodison Park, Liverpool.

Edson Arantes do Nascimento, or Pelé, will always be associated with Nº 10 and it is the dream of most Brazilian youngsters to wear the famous shirt, but it all started through good fortune.

The legend dates back to the 1958 World Cup, when Brazil failed to assign numbers to the squad submitted, leading FIFA to do it for them. So it was that goalkeeper Gilmar was given Nº 3, right winger Garrincha and left winger Mário Zagallo received Nº 11 and Nº 7 respectively – the opposite to the usual system – and 17-year-old Pelé was given 10, despite being a reserve at the outset of the tournament.

Given his chance for the third group game against the Soviet Union, he would go on to score six goals in four games, culminating in the 5-2 final win against the hosts, Sweden.

He was named as the Best Young Player at the tournament and went on to wear 10 for the remainder of his career, including further World Cup finals in 1962 and 1970.

So began a mystique around the Brazilian Nº 10, which has been worn by the likes of: Rivellino, Zico, Rivaldo, Ronaldinho, Kaká and Neymar.

Country
Brazil

Typeface
Sewn

Year
1966

Photography
Art Rickerby

10

The England Nº 1 shirt worn by the late Gordon Banks as the country won the 1966 World Cup.

A red number, as on the white outfield shirts, was used. Banks also had a blue change shirt with a white number — this was worn against Poland in England's last game before the World Cup but it wasn't required in the tournament.

Country
England

Typeface
Sewn

Year
1966

0

12

345

6789

August 27, 1994 is a significant day in Celtic's history.

The Bhoys won 2-0 against Rangers at Ibrox but their Glasgow rivals would go on to win a seventh straight Premier Division title. The lasting significance of the game comes from Celtic's kit: having worn shirts without numbers on their backs for so long, this signalled an irrevocable change.

Celtic didn't wear any numbers until a friendly against Sparta Rotterdam in May 1960, when they were writ large on the front and back of their shorts – numbers would be added to their change shirts but the club didn't want to spoil the famous hoops.

So it was that the famous Lisbon Lions won the 1967 European Cup against Inter Milan with numberless shirts.

They were forced to conform to a UEFA edict regarding shirt numbers in 1975 and, oddly, in a 1985 game at Hibernian the Celts wore a European-spec kit set with numbers on their backs. That was an isolated domestic incident until 1994, when the Scottish League told the club that it was time to fall into line. For the first two games of 1994-95, Celtic tried to test the definition of 'shirt numbers' by wearing them on their sleeves but the governing body clarified the meaning and the derby at Ibrox saw history created.

Club
Celtic F.C.

Typeface
Sewn

Year
1967

Club
Los Angeles Wolves

Typeface
Sewn

Year
1967

Club
Kansas City Spurs

Typeface
Sewn

Year
1968

Club
Detroit Cougars

Typeface
Sewn

Year
1968

Perhaps unsurprisingly, given the influence of Major League Baseball and the National Football League (NFL), the United Soccer Association and North American Soccer League (NASL) were ahead of the pack in terms of typography.

Early examples of shorts' numbering (popularised by Chelsea in England) featured, while the massive numbers on the front make the shirts appear to be worn the wrong way round.

The United Soccer Association only lasted one season before merging with the National Professional Soccer League (NPSL) to form the NASL. To help get the new venture off the ground, English clubs travelled over during the summer months and played under American names — for example, Wolverhampton Wanderers became the Los Angeles Wolves and Dundee United were known as Dallas Tornado.

NPSL side Baltimore Bays — represented by West Ham United — created history in 1967 with names on shirts. It's not hard to imagine that the angular lettering was inspired by the NFL, and a similar influence followed when the Premier League introduced names on shirts in 1993 [p112].

Club
Baltimore Bays

Typeface
Sewn

Year
1967-68

Photography
Dave Morrison

Club
Cagliari Calcio

Typeface
Sewn

Year
1969

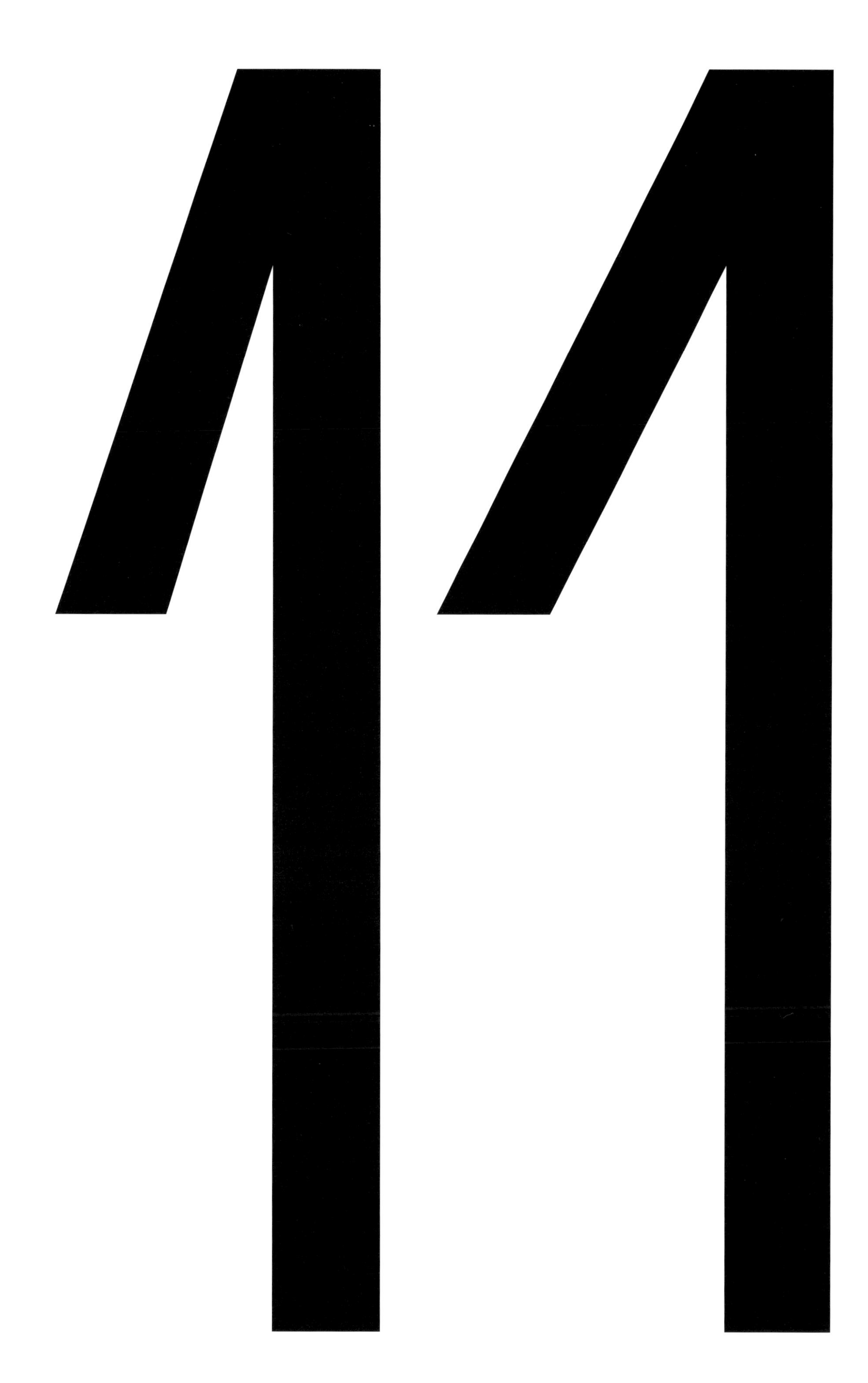

1970
1980

Digitalisation of Czechoslovakia's quirky, stitched-on numbers at the 1970 Mexico World Cup. The image opposite shows England striker Jeff Astle in a high-kicking duel with Czechoslovakia's Vladimír Hrivnák (Nº 14) during the game.

England wore specially-made Aertex shirts for greater breathability in the Mexican heat and the decision was made to have sky-blue change shirts to better reflect the sun. However, viewers on black-and-white televisions complained about the similarity of the blue with the Czechs' white kit and so, when England needed to change again, against West Germany in the quarter-finals, they opted for the more traditional red.

Country
Czechoslovakia

Typeface
Sewn

Year
1970

Photography
Keystone/Stringer

0
12
345
6789

14
VIVA

A close-up of the teabag-like Aertex material. This would again be used by England in tours in 1973 and 1974, with Umbro providing it as an option for club sides later in the decade.

Country
England

Typeface
Sewn

Year
1970

6

Though they failed to win a game, Morocco left their mark at the 1970 World Cup as they became the first country to wear numbers on their shorts at the competition.

The image shows Nº 4 Moulay Khassouni in action against Peru. For the next World Cup in West Germany in 1974, FIFA would mandate all competing countries to have shorts numbers.

Country
Morocco

Typeface
Sewn

Year
1970

Photography
Rolls Press

4

Country
El Salvador

Typeface
Sewn

Year
1970

Club
Generic jersey

Typeface
Sewn

Year
1970

Robert Frederick Chelsea 'Bobby' Moore was captain of West Ham United from 1962-74 and was aged just 22 when he skippered England for the first time in 1963.

In three consecutive seasons, he captained teams to win trophies at Wembley—the 1964 FA Cup and 1965 European Cup Winners' Cup with West Ham and of course the 1966 World Cup with England.

The composed, gentlemanly centre-back is regarded as one of the greatest players of all-time and Pelé recognised Moore as the best defender he ever played against.

After his death from cancer in March 1993, West Ham United played without a Nº 6 for their next home game against Wolverhampton Wanderers—Ian Bishop started the game wearing 12—and the club permanently retired the Nº 6 in August 2008. Matthew Upson was the last player to wear the number for the club, switching to 15 for 2008-09.

Club
West Ham United F.C.

Typeface
Sewn

Year
1970

Photography
Bob Sports

Country
Bulgaria

Typeface
Custom

Year
1970

Country
Cyprus

Typeface
Sewn

Year
1970

Country
Switzerland

Typeface
Sewn

Year
1970

Country
Greece

Typeface
Sewn

Year
1970

Country
USSR

Typeface
Sewn

Year
1971

Country
Austria

Typeface
Sewn

Year
1972

On October 10, 1972, France hosted the USSR in a World Cup qualifier in Paris. While the game itself was not of huge significance, it was noteworthy from a kit point of view in that the hosts wore numbers on the front of their shirts.

This practice had been seen in the USA and was adopted in the Coupe de France from 1970-71 onwards. Those numerals were produced by a sports manufacturing company called Somms and they were also called upon by the French Federation to provide the digits for the national team.

It's impossible to say for certain, but the distinctive Somms style makes this one of the first 'designed' numbersets. In addition, the front and back numbers all carried the Somms wordmark, which was almost definitely a first.

It meant that, unusually, three brands were represented on the France kit for the game — adidas made the shirts and Le Coq Sportif produced the shorts.

So far ahead of its time was this practice, that it died out again in France in the early 1980s, and Euro 92 would be the first major international tournament in which players had numbers on their shirt-fronts.

456789

SOMMS SOMMS SOMMS SOMMS SOMMS SOMMS

456789

SOMMS SOMMS SOMMS SOMMS SOMMS SOMMS

Country
France

Typeface
Custom

Year
1972

The 1974 World Cup was noteworthy for the various differing number fonts employed, including the first sighting of the famous adidas style, which incorporated the three stripes with which the company is synonymous. This type of numbering, which bears similarities with the branding for the 1968 Olympic Games in Mexico, was still used by the Republic of Ireland at the 1990 World Cup.

This is a digitalisation of the number 16 worn by Argentina's Francisco Sá.

Club & Countries
Names & numbers for all adidas teams

Typeface
Custom

Year
1974

Design
adidas

0 1 2 3 4 5 6 7 8 9

Country
Netherlands

Typeface
Custom

Year
1974

The Netherlands squad for the 1974 World Cup was numbered alphabetically by surname – with one notable exception.

Having missed the early part of 1970-71 due to a groin problem, Ajax's Johan Cruyff returned for the game against PSV on October 30.

Midfielder Gerrie Mühren went to the kit hamper to get his regular Nº 7 only to find that the kitman, known as 'Uncle Jan' (whose wife laundered the strip) had mislaid it. Cruyff, who had usually worn 9, told Mühren to take that and the striker opted to wear 14 instead. Ajax won and the following week Cruyff suggested to Mühren that they retain their 'lucky' numbers.

Cruyff would wear 14 as Ajax won three consecutive European Cup finals in 1971, 1972 and 1973, and such was his influence, he was allowed to buck the alphabetical trend for the World Cup in Argentina and keep his favoured number. In 'normal' international games, and after he joined Barcelona, Cruyff would have to wear Nº 9, but when engaging in pre-match visualisation techniques, he always had 14 on his back.

Ajax retired the Nº 14 shirt on Cruyff's 60th birthday, April 25, 2007.

4

A 24-year World Cup run began at the 1974 tournament as the host country, West Germany, premiered the distinctive 3D keyline-shadow style, the first example of this numbering.

With iconic captain Franz Beckenbauer wearing the Nº 5 shirt and Gerd Müller scoring four goals in seven games with Nº 13 on his back, Die Mannschaft ended a 20-year wait for the title. When they won for the third time at Italia 90, similar numbering was still in use and would remain the font of choice for World Cups until France 98.

Country
West-Germany

Typeface
Custom

Year
1974

5

Following the lead of Morocco in 1970, shorts-numbering was made mandatory for all competing sides at the 1974 World Cup. While Argentina had the adidas three-stripe style on their shirts [p56], the numbering on their right legs was completely different: on the left is the Nº 8 carried by Enrique Chazarreta.

Country
Argentina

Typeface
Custom

Year
1974

Italy's shorts numbering did match those on the backs of their shirts. This distinctive Nº 8 was worn by Fabio Capello, who scored the country's only goal of the finals in their 2-1 defeat to Poland.

Country
Italy

Typeface
Custom

Year
1974

As the 1960s gave way to the 1970s, experiments continued with regards to team presentation in North America.

Dallas Tornado (left) had an early example of two-tone numbering, where the digits were outlined in a different colour, helping to further tie in with the team's own identity.

San Jose Earthquakes (right) carried the name of their city vertically down the sleeves of their shirts, while there was an unusual instance of a player's first name and surname being on the back. Even more unusual was the split style, which meant the surname was covered if the shirt was tucked in!

Club
Dallas Tornado

Typeface
Custom

Year
1974

Photography
Dave Morrison

SAN JOSE

Club
San Jose Earthquakes

Typeface
Custom

Year
1975

Photography
Dave Morrison

Throughout the 1970s and up to the mid-1990s, adidas's individual licensees in each country were allowed a certain amount of leeway in terms of modifying designs with unique flourishes.

One example is Switzerland adopting a more angular version of the three-stripe numbering font. They would use this until 1990, when the country's association entered into a deal with little known company Blacky. Later versions of this numbering included the adidas Trefoil at the base.

Country
Switzerland

Typeface
Custom

Year
1975

Design
adidas

Club
San Diego Jaws

Typeface
Custom

Year
1976

Photography
Dave Morrison

In the USA, just below Major League Soccer, is the United Soccer League Championship, which is where the Tampa Bay Rowdies reside, having previously played in the second iteration of the North American Soccer League (NASL).

Of course, the first incarnation of the Rodies was a standout name in the original NASL and, after that league folded, the team played on until 1996, the last surviving franchise to still be in action.

The new Rowdies had to endure a long legal wrangle to acquire the name and logo of the previous club. The logo and the mascot, Ralph Rowdie, a fictional moustachioed character – who gives his name to 'Ralph's Mob', an independent supporters' group – were the work of artist Scott Ross.

"They already had an ad design agency in Atlanta working on their PR stuff and I was given a rough sketch of a logo and asked to 'clean it up a little and make it less strange-looking,'" he said. "I reworked it but still kept the original idea for the one-colour version. Then I came up with the two-colour version using the colours of their uniform. Originally, the letters were very close together and all the ends of the letters were longer. I think originally someone used the look of the psychedelic Haight-Ashbury Fillmore posters for the lettering but it was highly unreadable. When I did the original character logo, I added the border around the lettering so I could add a trim colour. I messed with all the letters to make it more readable and more commercial even though it was pretty unique for the time or any time."

In addition to the uniqueness was the fact that the front and back numbers, created by Umbro, tied in perfectly with the 'Rowdies' wordmark.

Club
Tampa Bay Rowdies

Typeface
Custom

Year
1976

Logo design
Scott Ross

Photography
Dave Morrison

Country
Team Hawaii

Typeface
Custom

Year
1977

Photography
Dave Morrison

George Best is regarded as the creator of the legend of the Manchester United Nº 7 shirt but, while he did wear it in the 1968 European Cup final win over Benfica, he wore Nº 11 in more than half of the 470 games he played for the Red Devils.

Therefore, it wasn't a surprise that he should also wear 11 for NASL side the Los Angeles Aztecs when he joined them in 1976.

The team logo was similar to another, which was coincidentally adopted in the same year as Best joined – that of Japanese gaming company Sega. The Sega insignia is believed to derive from the Yagi Double typeface, developed by Robert Trogman and published by his company FotoStar in 1968.

The concept of the nameplate originated in baseball, where player trades were common and jerseys would be recycled through a Major League club's farm system. With so many different players wearing the same jersey, it was easier to have the nameplate to unstitch rather than having to remove each individual letter.

Incidentally, Best would later play for the Fort Lauderdale Strikers and, rather usually wore the Nº 3 for them, though he would revert to 11 for his time at the San Jose Earthquakes.

Club
Los Angeles Aztecs

Typeface
Custom

Year
1977

Photography
Dave Morrison

Country
Sweden

Typeface
Custom

Year
1978

Design
adidas

Swedish attacker, Benny Wendt, wore Nº 11 in the 1978 World Cup.

Independent of Switzerland's change in numbering [p66] was another alteration to the original 1974 style, which saw it become more humanist and less geometric.

In 1979, the Vancouver Whitecaps effected one of the first 'holistic' designs, utilising the same font for both the team's logo and shirt numbers.

Produced by Admiral and carrying patriotic red maple leaves on the sleeves, the shirts had a new colour-scheme in white and two-tone blue.

The baseball practice of having the team name on the home jersey and city name on the away jersey was adopted and both were rendered in a customised version of ITC Bauhaus, with the front back and side numbers in the same font. Oddly, however, the names on the back didn't follow suit.

Designed in 1975, ITC Bauhaus went on to be featured on numerous shirts, including AS Roma in 1998, Real Madrid in 2003 and across adidas's roster at the 2006 World Cup [p180].

Club
Vancouver Whitecaps

Typeface
ITC Bauhaus
(Numbers,
customised)

Year
1979

Photography
Dave Morrison

KENYON
6

Scotland's friendly game at home to Peru in September 1979 marked a notable first.

Research by Simon Shakeshaft for *Programme Monthly* magazine reveals that, after the anthems, the Scottish players removed their tracksuit tops to reveal what had been a well-kept secret – they had names above their numbers.

Only a handful of people linked to the SFA and kit manufacturers Umbro knew of secretary Ernie Walker's plan to 'Americanise' Scotland's match shirts, becoming the first international team to carry players' names. Walker, who had come up with the idea after watching NASL games while in the USA, noted that "they will be commonplace in the future" and that in 20 years' time, "as likely as not, club sides will probably have followed suit". This was amazing foresight, but unfortunately for the pioneers Walker and the Scottish FA, they weren't to be rewarded with the huge revenue streams that names and numbers on shirts realised for clubs and national associations today.

Country
Scotland

Typeface
Custom

Year
1979

The idea, described in the programme by Walker as "to improve communication between the field of play and the spectators" — similar to the aims of Dave Calderhead and Herbert Chapman when Chelsea and Arsenal piloted numbering a half-century earlier [p12] — but such innovations are not without teething problems.

Two types of letter fonts were used on three different shirt styles, with Umbro's larger capitalized letter font most commonly applied. Because the SFA were initially unsure they would be allowed to use the names in competitive qualifying matches, a standard retail shop smaller letter, first seen in Euro qualifier against Portugal in March 1980, was also used.

The difference can be seen on the two shirts illustrated: Kenny Burns' Nº 6 shirt from that first game against Peru — with old-style cloth numbers — and another Burns shirt, Nº 4, worn against Northern Ireland — with a new flock outline number font — in March 1981.

Country
Scotland

Typeface
Cooper Black (Names)

Year
1981

1980
1990

Club
Nottingham Forest F.C.

Typeface
Cooper Black (Names) &
Custom adidas (Numbers)

Year
1980

The Cooper Black font seen on the Scotland shirts in 1981 had actually premiered on another team's kit the previous winter.

While Nottingham Forest had won the European Cup in 1979, they opted against taking part in the World Club Cup, with their place taken by beaten finalists Malmö FF. A year on though, and with the cup retained, Brian Clough's men featured in the first one-legged final, against Nacional of Uruguay in Tokyo.

The game also marked another first in that the Forest players had their names above their numbers, albeit in a rather incongruous meeting of fonts.

John Robertson, who wore Nº 11, often struggled with fitness but his natural talent meant that Clough made allowances. When right winger Martin O'Neill complained that almost all of Forest's play went down the left, Clough's retort was: "And so it should go down the left-hand side. Because that lad's a bloody genius."

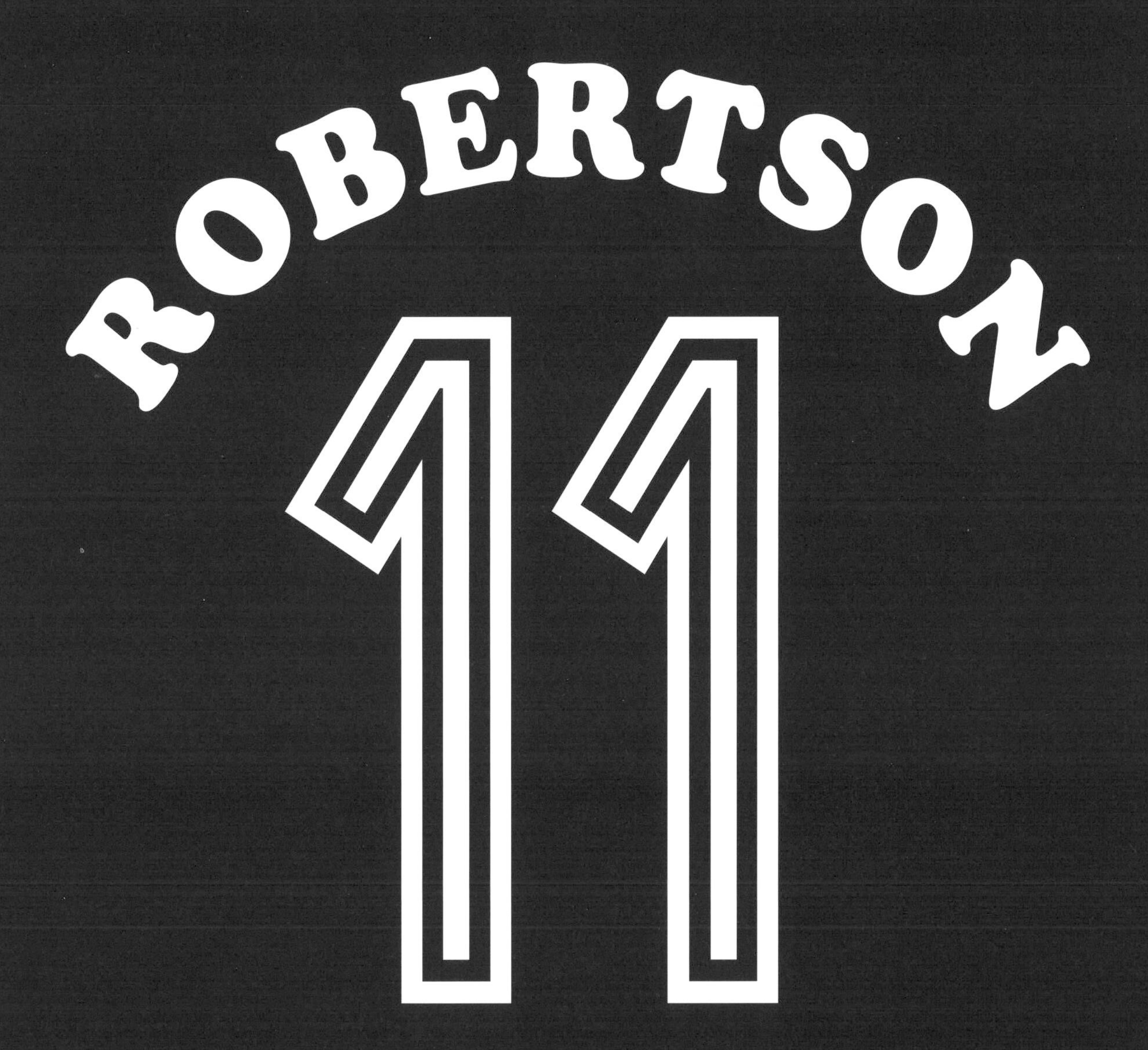
ROBERTSON
11

McDERMOTT
10

Liverpool declined to take part in the Intercontinental Cup in 1977 and 1978, meaning that the 1981 event against Flamengo in Tokyo's National Stadium was their first appearance and the game also marked another significant departure.

As with Forest the previous year, Liverpool also had the players' names above their numbers, though in a style more in keeping with the digits.

While the English grip on the European Cup remained tight with Aston Villa's win in 1982, they opted against names on shirts for their clash with Peñarol.

Club
Liverpool F.C.

Typeface
Custom

Year
1981

Club
Club Atlético
Independiente

Typeface
Bodoni Ultra Condensed
(customised)

Year
1981

Manchester United's first link-up with adidas came in 1980 and their first season together saw the three-stripe numbers [p56] used, but the German firm came up with a new style in 1981.

This slimmed design featured the adidas Trefoil at the bottom of the numbers, but after a third-placed finish in 1981-82 saw United qualify for the 1982-83 UEFA Cup, they were forced to modify the numbers for European competition.

As well as having to remove the adidas wordmark from under the Trefoil on the front of the shirts, United weren't permitted to brandish the logo on their numbers. The quick fix was to cover it with tape.

This Nº 3 shirt was worn by Arthur Albiston against Juventus in 1983-84.

Club
Manchester United F.C.

Typeface
Custom

Year
1981

Design
adidas

Photography
Rob Hurst

3

Country
Argentina

Typeface
Custom

Year
1982

Photography
Mark Leech

Like the Netherlands [p58], Argentina employed an alphabetical numbering system at the 1974 World Cup – with the exception of their three goalkeepers, who wore 1, 21 and 22.

For the 1978 competition, which La Albiceleste hosted and won, the AFA went fully alphabetical, with first-choice goalkeeper Ubaldo Fillol wearing 5 (his opposite number in the final, Jan Jongbloed of the Netherlands, wore 8 – the Dutch had dispensed with alphabetical numbering, but some of the survivors from 1974 kept the same numbers).

Osvaldo 'Ossie' Ardiles wore № 2 in 1978, with Norberto Alonso wearing № 1. Four years later in Spain it would be Ardiles carrying the figure usually worn by the goalkeeper (Fillol was № 7 in 1982).

Ardiles and Diego Maradona are pictured before the game against Brazil on July 2, 1982 – Ardiles had his number on the right leg of his shorts but all of the other players had theirs on the left leg.

Admiral's arrival on the kit market in the early 1970s brought a sea-change as designs became bold and adventurous.

From 1978, an angular, slab-serif font was introduced, possibly influenced by American football.

England failed to qualify for the 1974 and 1978 World Cups, meaning that Euro 80 and the 1982 World Cup were the only major finals in which Admiral kits were worn by the country.

Country
England

Typeface
Custom

Year
1982

Digitalisation of Belgium defender Michel Renquin's 1982 World Cup squad number. As well as England, Admiral also provided the kit for Belgium at the competition, but their numbering differed in that each figure was made up of a series of stripes.

Country
Belgium

Typeface
Custom

Year
1982

10

Country
Argentina

Typeface
Custom

Year
1986

As we saw on page 84, Argentina's Ossie Ardiles wore Nº 2 at the 1978 World Cup and Nº 1 four years later as the country numbered its players alphabetically, but there was one exception for the latter competition in Spain.

According to the order, Diego Maradona should have been wearing 12 with midfielder Patricio Hernández given Nº 10, but Maradona convinced either Hernández or the Argentinian FA to allow the pair to swap.

For Mexico 86, Maradona was again allowed to override the alphabetical practice and he was joined in this by captain Daniel Passarella (Nº 6) and Jorge Valdano (Nº 11) as La Albiceleste regained the title won on home soil eight years previously.

The shadow of Maradona looms large over the Nº 10 for all of his former teams, though Napoli have avoided comparisons by retiring the shirt. For Argentina, a number of starlets have been tagged as 'the New Maradona', with only Lionel Messi really able to live up to the billing.

Prior to the 2002 World Cup, Argentina sought to retire Nº 10 as well, submitting a list featuring players numbered 1-9 and 11-24, but FIFA refused to allow this. Ariel Ortega wore Nº 10, as he had in 1998, while Juan Román Riquelme was bestowed with the honour in 2006. For each of the three subsequent World Cups, 2010, 2014 and 2018, Messi has been the Nº 10, but the country remains waiting for a third title.

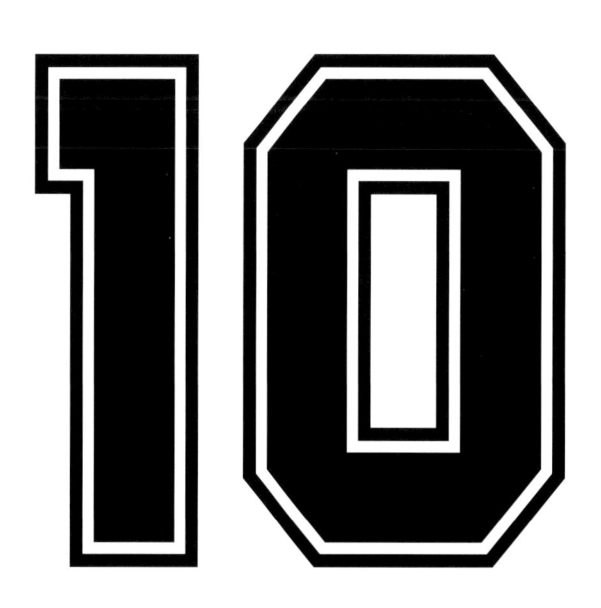

This Leeds United change shirt had a three-year lifespan from 1989-92, taking in title wins in the old Division 2 and the old Division 1 (the last champions of England before the Premier League). However, this is one of the rarest versions.

Used in 1989-90, this shirt worn by David Batty is a prime example of how a nice design can be trumped by functionality.

The number style was made up of a series of horizontal lines, with the Umbro double-diamond logo created by breaking those lines. However, Leeds had only used this numbering twice before the Football League asked for it to be changed due to visibility issues.

A solid version was used for the remainder of that season with a more rounded, traditional font on show for 1990-91 and 1991-92.

Club
Leeds United F.C.

Typeface
Custom

Year
1989

Design
Umbro

1990
2000

England's 1990 World Cup home shirts boasted magnificent, bold, red slab-serif numbers, similar to those accompanying the Three Lions at Euro 88. Paul Gascoigne wore Nº 19 for Bobby Robson's side.

The unpredictable Geordie was one of Italia 90's leading lights. His trickery dominated the group match against the Netherlands and his vision and passing helped England eliminate Cameroon in the quarter-final. Gazza's tears after picking up a yellow card in the semi-final against West Germany – meaning he would miss the final had England reached it – made him a global icon.

It was one of only two major finals Gascoigne played in. Injury ruled him out of Euro 92 and England failed to qualify for the 1994 World Cup. He appeared in Euro 96, wearing the Nº 8 with which he was more associated, but wasn't included in the squad for France 98.

When England squad numbers are announced for World Cups, the issuing of Nº 19 draws the greatest interest, outside of the 1-11 numbers. The players to wear it since Gascoigne have been: Les Ferdinand (1998), Joe Cole (2002), Aaron Lennon (2006), Jermain Defoe (2010), Raheem Sterling (2014) and Marcus Rashford (2018).

Country
England

Typeface
Custom

Year
1990

Design
Umbro

Club
Generic jersey

Typeface
Custom

Year
1991

Design
Umbro

Club
Tottenham Hotspur F.C.

Typeface
Custom

Year
1991

Design
Umbro

3D numbering was firmly in vogue at Euro 92. Germany (left), competing as a united country for the first time since reunification, continued with the same font West Germany had had since 1974, while France (right), had a slightly different style despite also being outfitted by adidas. The Netherlands (middle) used a broader version on their Lotto kits.

Countries
Germany, Netherlands & France

Typefaces
Custom

Year
1992

Design
adidas, Lotto & adidas

7

The early 1990s saw the inclusion of makers' logos on numbers become more common as other companies followed the lead of adidas.

However, the German firm still found the same problems as the 1980s when it came to European competition [p86] and so the Trefoil on the memorable Manchester United change shirt was hazily scribbled over.

During the lifespan of this font, adidas introduced the 'Equipment' logo in 1991 and so both the Trefoil and the new insignia appeared on the distinctive numbers.

Clubs
Manchester United F.C.
& Arsenal F.C.

Typefaces
Custom

Year
1992 & 1993

Design
adidas

No, you haven't lost your balance – this is how Borussia Dortmund's numbers were presented in the 1993-94 season.

The easy assumption is that this was Nike looking to mark themselves out as different (Dortmund, along with Paris Saint-Germain and Monaco, were among their first big European contracts), but this wasn't a first in Germany. Three years previously, St. Pauli had utilised a similar concept on the back of their Puma shirts.

Given that Dortmund's experiment only lasted a season, we can surmise that legibility was not ideal and there is a reason why practically every other team in the world has numbers laid out vertically.

In Germany, it's traditional for the team name to be rendered above the number – to this day, quite a few Bundesliga sides have the player names below the digits for that reason – but here Dortmund had it to the side. While Futura was the font used on the home shirts, Helvetica was the choice for the away.

Club
Borussia Dortmund

Typeface
Custom

Year
1993

The second year of the Premier League, 1993-94, brought the advent of squad numbering for teams, following successful trials in both domestic finals in 1992-93 (each featuring Arsenal and Sheffield Wednesday).

For the first four years under the new system, clubs were given free rein on design once they complied with regulations on size and legibility.

This was also a period in which quite a few clubs sought to maximise income from replica shirts by producing kit in-house — Leicester City played in their own Fox Leisure brand from 1992-2000.

Club
Leicester City F.C.

Typeface
Helvetica Inserat (Names)

Year
1993

SPEED

Club
Leeds United F.C.

Typeface
Custom

Year
1993

SCHMEICHEL

1

Manchester United joined forces with Umbro in 1992, ushering in an era of great success for the club, beginning with the winning of the inaugural Premier League. The first kits under the new deal remain memorable while the new American-inspired slab-serif number font was adopted by the rest of the Umbro stable and is one of the stand-out styles of the 1990s.

Club
Manchester United F.C.

Typeface
Custom

Year
1993

Design
Umbro

CANTONA

Today, there is a huge aura and mystique around the Manchester United Nº 7 shirt but much of the legend is a fairly recent construction, reverse-engineered in the wake of Eric Cantona's impact and carried from there.

As mentioned on page 67, George Best wore Nº 11 far more than 7 for United and Bryan Robson had developed his affinity for the number at West Bromwich Albion. When the Premier League introduced squad numbers in 1993-94, Cantona was given Nº 7 with Robson allocated Nº 12, but with 1-11 still in force in European competitions, Cantona switched to Nº 9 for four Champions League qualifying games to allow Robson to wear his preferred digit.

Kit design became bolder in the 1990s, with goalkeeper shirts allowing for a real pushing of the creative envelope.

Umbro experimented with triangles in 1991-92 and chalkstripes in 1992-93 before things really took off in 1993 and other manufacturers such as Asics and later adidas also joined in the fun.

At the 1994 World Cup in the USA, four different Umbro goalkeeper shirts really caught the eye, but they weren't part of the Manchester company's 'standard' offerings.

Mexico goalkeeper Jorge Campos appeared in a different kit for each of his country's games, all four of the retina-scorching variety, subscribing to the theory that such bright explosions of colour were distracting for opposition forwards. This was well ahead of its time.

Particularly impressive was the fact that Campos designed these kits himself. This sense of experimental flair contributed to his cult status.

Campos also appeared at France 98 but in more sedate offerings, though he did sometimes opt to wear the Mexico outfield away kit. Even today, the designs from a quarter-century ago ensure he is remembered, though he did have an impressive portfolio of on-field achievements.

As well as keeping goal, Campos sometimes played as a striker, scoring 34 goals in two spells with Mexican side UNAM PUMAs. While he played in goal during his time with Major League Soccer side LA Galaxy, he did opt to wear the № 9 shirt most often associated with the centre-forward position.

Country
Mexico

Typeface
Hobo

Year
1994

CAMPOS
1

Umbro took over the Brazil kit contract from Topper in 1991. Initially, a unique rounded font was used, but by the time of the 1994 World Cup they had shifted to angular shadow style.

DUNGA

Country
Brazil

Typefaces
Block Gothic Condensed (Names)
& Custom (Numbers)

Year
1994

Brazil won the World Cup for the first time in 24 years, while defending champions Germany continued to keep faith with the keyline shadow, which was celebrating its 20th anniversary.

MÖLLER

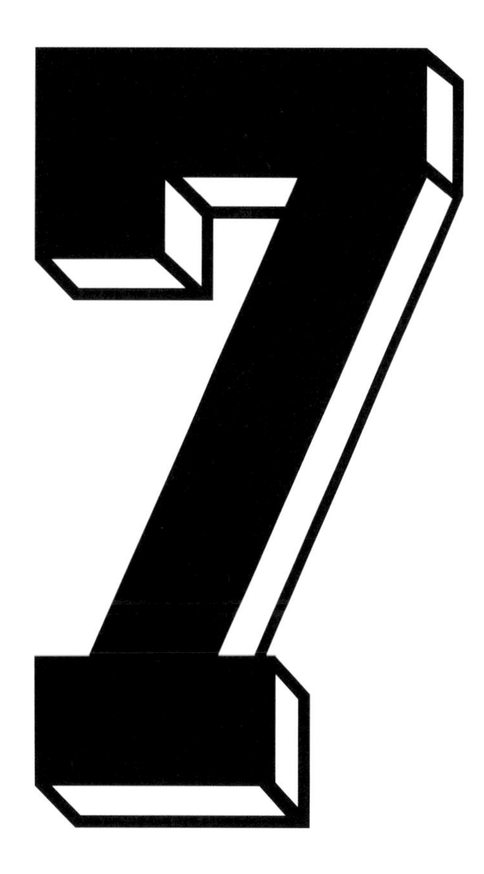

Country
Germany

Typefaces
Futura Condensed (Names, distorted) & Custom (Numbers)

Year
1994

It wasn't all squared fonts at USA 94 though, with beaten finalists Italy having a memorable style, but it may not be to the taste of design purists.

Taking a standard font and distorting and stretching it can save the time involved in creating one from scratch — Italy did it with two, one for the names and one for the numbers.

Country
Italy

Typefaces
VAG (Names, distorted)
& Crillee (Numbers)

Year
1994

R.BAGGIO

KLINSMANN

While the keyline shadow would remain in use by Germany at World Cups until 1998, their Euro 96 kits betrayed the first hint of a move away from what had become such an identifiable look.

As with Italy two years previously, they employed two different fonts on the back of their shirts.

Country
Germany

Typefaces
Times New Roman (Names)
& Footlight (Numbers)

Year
1996

Peacock blue was a brand-new addition to the England kit palette in 1995, featuring on the strip which would be used when the country hosted Euro 96.

Harking back to something first seen in the NASL [p64], Umbro opted for two-tone slab-serif and lettering, navy with peacock blue on the home kit, which was introduced during the 1994-95 season.

Also launched in the middle of that campaign was the blue and white Manchester United third kit, which had yellow numbers and letters trimmed in black, and the concept would be expanded to more Umbro club kits, and the indigo-blue England change strip, in 1995-96.

Country
England

Typeface
Custom

Year
1996

Design
Umbro

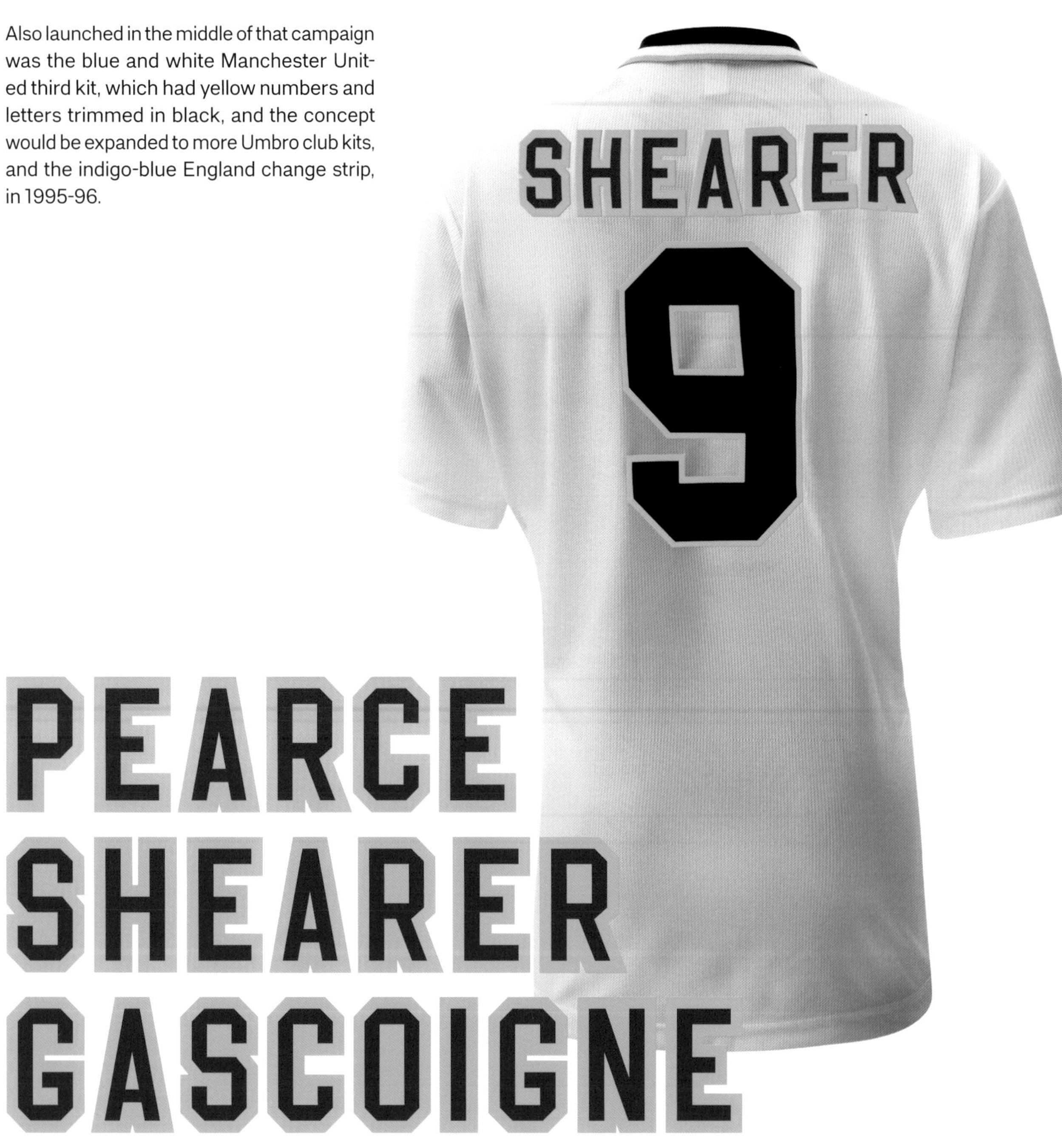

Club
Manchester United F.C.

Typeface
Custom

Year
1996

Design
Umbro

For the fifth season of the Premier League, 1997-98, it was decided that a common font should be used by all teams, thereby ensuring a royalty for the league on all numbered shirts sold.

The new typeface, created by Sporting iD and produced in Kinsale, Co. Cork in Ireland by Chris Kay Ltd., was a squeezed version of Optima.

Teams were still free to use their own fonts in the domestic cups and European competitions. However, in the case of the latter, the Premier League numbers often remained, albeit without the 'lion' logo.

A B C D E F G H I J K L M N
O P Q R S T U V W X Y Z

01234
56789

Brand
Premier League

Typeface
Optima (distorted)

Year
1997

Design
Sporting iD

TM
THE F.A. PREMIER LEAGUE
© FAPL 1996

BERGKAMP

The last season of the original pan-Premier League numbering, 2006-07, was Arsenal's first without Dennis Bergkamp, the Dutchman having retired after 11 years at Highbury.

Just before the summer 2006 transfer window closed, Arsenal swapped Ashley Cole for William Gallas and the club initially announced that the French international would wear the Nº 3 shirt which Cole had vacated.

GALLAS

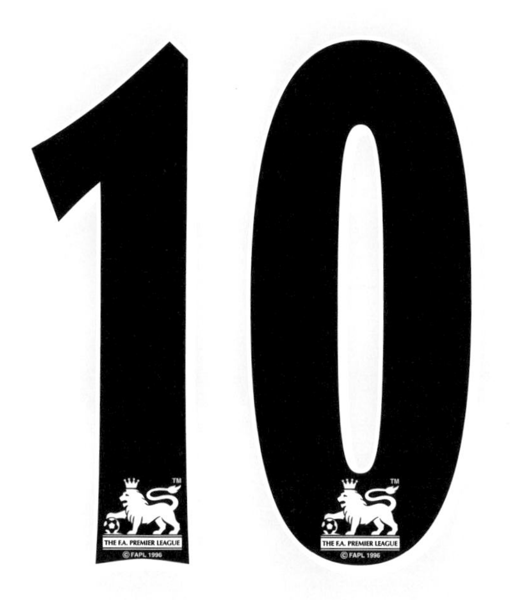

However, Gallas was uncomfortable with wearing 3 as he had been assigned the number against his will at Chelsea when Michael Ballack arrived and was given the Nº 13 that the defender had had.

The solution was to instead switch Gallas to Nº 10, with Arsenal manager Arsène Wenger saying: "I thought it might be a good idea to give 10 to a defender. A striker would suffer with the comparison with Dennis."

Club
Inter Milan

Typefaces
Block Gothic (Names) &
Custom (Numbers)

Year
1997

Club
Palmeiras

Typeface
Custom

Year
1998

012

567

34

789

Club
Real Madrid C.F.

Typeface
Custom

Year
1998

Country
Netherlands

Typeface
Custom

Year
1998

Design
Nike

OKOCHA

Country
Nigeria

Typeface
Din

Year
1998

KELME
Spanair
1.3

Club
RCD Mallorca

Typefaces
Custom

Year
1999

Coming off the back of good displays for Argentina in the 1998 World Cup, goalkeeper Carlos Roa was in superb form for Real Mallorca in 1998-99.

Having won the Copa del Rey the previous year, the club beat Barcelona in the Supercopa and then made it all the way to the final of the last-ever European Cup Winners' Cup, losing to Lazio at Villa Park.

A third-placed finish in La Liga was the club's highest and Roa played a big part in that, conceding 29 goals in 35 games, winning the Trofeo Ricardo Zamora, awarded to the goalkeeper with the lowest goals-to-games ratio.

Spanish league rules mandated that goalkeepers had to wear Nº 1, 13 or 25 and Roa had opted for the middle one of these options, placing a dot between the '1' and '3' — a member of the Seventh-day Adventist Church, he was paying tribute to the Holy Trinity and his belief in the existence of God, Jesus and the Holy Spirit in one.

At the age of 29, Roa was much sought-after in the summer of 1999 but instead, his religious beliefs led him to retire from football as he believed the world was about to end. Armageddon wasn't forthcoming though and Roa returned to see out his contract with Mallorca.

However, the Nº 13 shirt had been taken by Miki and Roa had to make do with the Nº 1, but he couldn't rediscover his previous form. In the summer of 2002, he joined Albacete, where he again donned Nº 13.

NEVILLE
CAMPBELL
ADAMS
BECKHAM
INCE
McMANAMA

Country
England

Typeface
Friz Quadrata (distorted)

Year
1999

Design
Sporting iD

SEAMAN
NEVILLE
OWEN

As well as the Premier League font, Sporting iD were also behind a new font for England in 1999, which was based on the Football Association's corporate typeface.

The 2002 World Cup was the first tournament where England wore non-red numbers on the white home shirt since 1954, with navy favoured by Umbro on this occasion. The highlight of the group stages was the 1-0 win over Argentina, with David Beckham scoring a penalty to atone for his sending-off against the Albiceleste in 1998.

However, draws with Sweden and Nigeria meant that England finished in second place in Group F, resulting in a last-16 clash with Brazil. The South American side won 2-1 and went on to win the competition for the fifth time.

SHEARER

N

Photography
AFP

BECKHAM
7
BECKHAM
7

ZAMORANO

1+8

Iván 'Bam Bam' Zamorano was a classic centre-forward, so it was no surprise that the Chilean should be bestowed with Nº 9 for Real Madrid when La Liga introduced squad numbers for the 1995-96 season.

A year later, Zamorano was Milan-bound, having signed for Internazionale. Serie A had also taken the squad-numbering plunge in 1995-96, with midfielder Felice Centofanti wearing Nº 9 for Inter, but his departure allowed Zamorano to take the shirt.

While Ronaldo arrived from Barcelona in 1997, he had to make do with Nº 10, but the signing of Roberto Baggio from Bologna in 1998 set in motion a chain-reaction. Though Baggio had been content to wear Nº 18 during his time with AC Milan, he now demanded his trademark Nº 10 and, to accommodate him, Ronaldo switched to Nº 9 with Zamorano moving to Nº 18.

However, 'Bam Bam' was allowed to make one amendment, with the inclusion of a small plus between the '1' and the '8', meaning he remained a Nº 9.

Club
Inter Milan

Typefaces
Trade Gothic (Names)
& VAG (Numbers)

Year
1999

2000
2010

Club
Real Madrid C.F.

Typeface
Stencil

Year
2000

Photography
Andrey Vasilvev (courtesy of PROsport magazine)

R. CARLOS

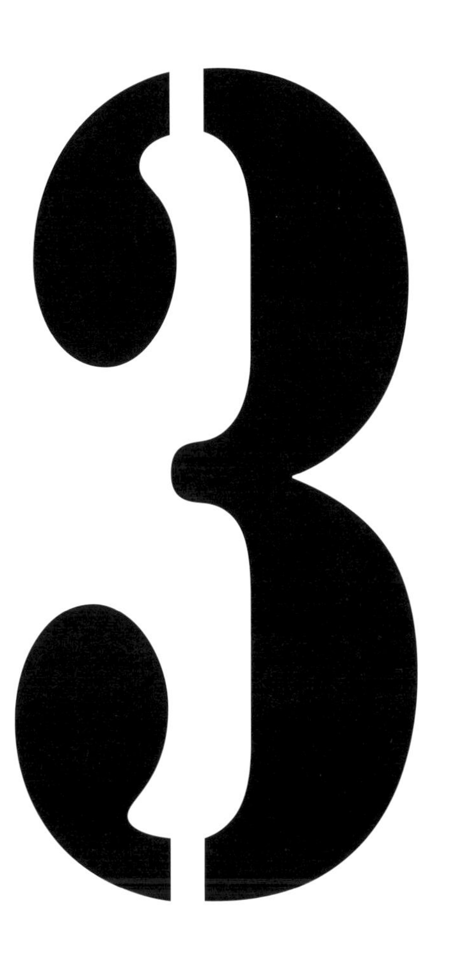

Sander Neijnens is a legendary Dutch typographer and his passion for football caused him to notice the unfitness for purpose of so many shirt number and name styles, making recognition much harder.

According to Neijnens, the key to good shirt numbers was to have them serifed, semi-bold and with a clear contrast between thick and thin. To back up these views, in 2002 he designed a set of classically proportioned Dutch-style figures, 'King', to invoke strength, flexibility and athletic power. This font was used by Willem II from Tilburg.

In 2004, Neijnens published a book on the subject, entitled *Shirt Numbers*.

1234567890

1234567890

1234567890

123457890

1234567890

Club
Football club Willem II Tilburg

Typeface
King

Year
2002

Design
Bladvulling

Designer
Sander Neijnens

Photography
Geert van Erven

SONG

During the early 2000s, PUMA pushed the envelope with their Cameroon kits, testing the strictness of the authorities' rules.

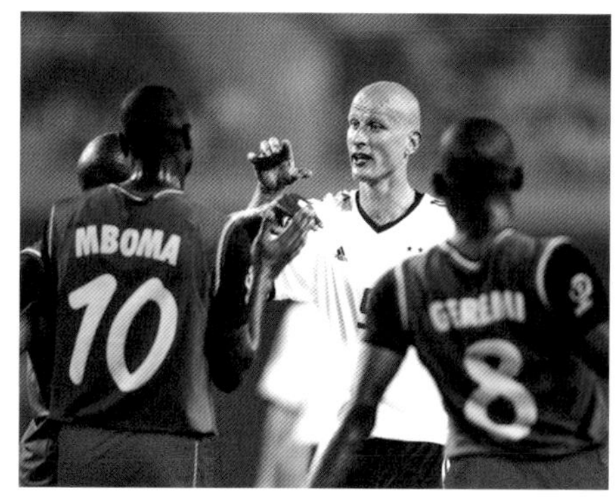

At the 2002 Africa Cup of Nations in Mali, the Indomitable Lions turned heads with a basketball-style sleeveless shirt and the new style didn't stop them winning a fourth title. However, by the time of that summer's World Cup in Japan and South Korea, FIFA insisted on a kit of a more traditional construction — otherwise, there would have been nowhere to put the competition patches. Black sleeves were added so as to retain the original visual from a distance.

For the Africa Cup of Nations in Tunisia in 2004, PUMA again looked to experimen and this time they produced one-piece garments rather than separate shirts and shorts.

12345
67890

FIFA President Sepp Blatter wasn't impressed: "It goes against the laws of the game. The rules are very clear, there is one shirt, one shorts and one socks. They cannot do it. You cannot play a game against the laws of the game. We are the guardians of the laws of the game — the laws are universal."

Cameroon continued to wear the kit during the competition but they couldn't retain their title, losing to Nigeria in the quarter-finals. FIFA fined Cameroon $154,000 (a fine paid by PUMA) and docked them six points for the 2006 World Cup qualifiers. After appeal, the points were restored, but Cameroon — back in shirts, shorts and socks — failed to qualify anyway.

Country
Cameroon

Typefaces
Futura (Names) &
Freestyle Script (Numbers)

Year
2002

66
Paul
Smith

This is as close as you'll get to a Paul Smith-designed football kit, a special edition of the England shirt worn in Japan and South Korea.

"For the 2002 World Cup we've made all the accessories for the England team, like the suitcases, wallets and cufflinks," he said.

"We've been asked a lot in the past to design kits, but I've always declined, because you're restricted by so many factors, usually the sponsors."

This was a period when Umbro were experimenting with a number of concepts. The red England away shirt produced for that World Cup was reversible, allowing supporters to wear it inside-out as a navy blue t-shirt.

Country
England

Typeface
Friz Quadrata (distorted)

Year
2002

Design
Paul Smith

RONALDO

99

ACM
1899

ACM
1899

In 2004, AC Milan's kits sported a new gold name and number style, created by Sporting iD at the invitation of kit manufacturers adidas.

This popular style was to remain unchanged for four years, taking in the 2007 Champions League final win over Liverpool as the Rossoneri gained revenge for the defeat in Istanbul two years previously.

While Ronaldo was with Milan by this stage, having joined during the winter transfer window in 2006-07, he was cup-tied for the Champions League, having played for Real Madrid in the competition in the earlier part of that season.

Though strongly associated with the Nº 9, it is not all that he wore. He had Nº 10 in his first season at Inter Milan and when he joined Real in 2002 he initially took Nº 11 as Fernando Morientes had 9, but the Brazilian took Nº 9 when Morientes departed the following year.

When Ronaldo pitched up at the San Siro for the second time – the first player to play for Barcelona, Real Madrid, AC Milan and Inter Milan – the AC Milan Nº 9 shirt was held by Filippo Inzaghi and so he opted for Nº 99.

After Milan, Ronaldo returned to Brazil to finish his career with Corinthians. While he wore Nº 9, he did also don Nº 99 to celebrate the São Paulo club's 99th anniversary.

Club
A.C. Milan

Typeface
Custom

Year
2004

Design
Sporting iD

Designer
Anthony Barnett

BALLACK

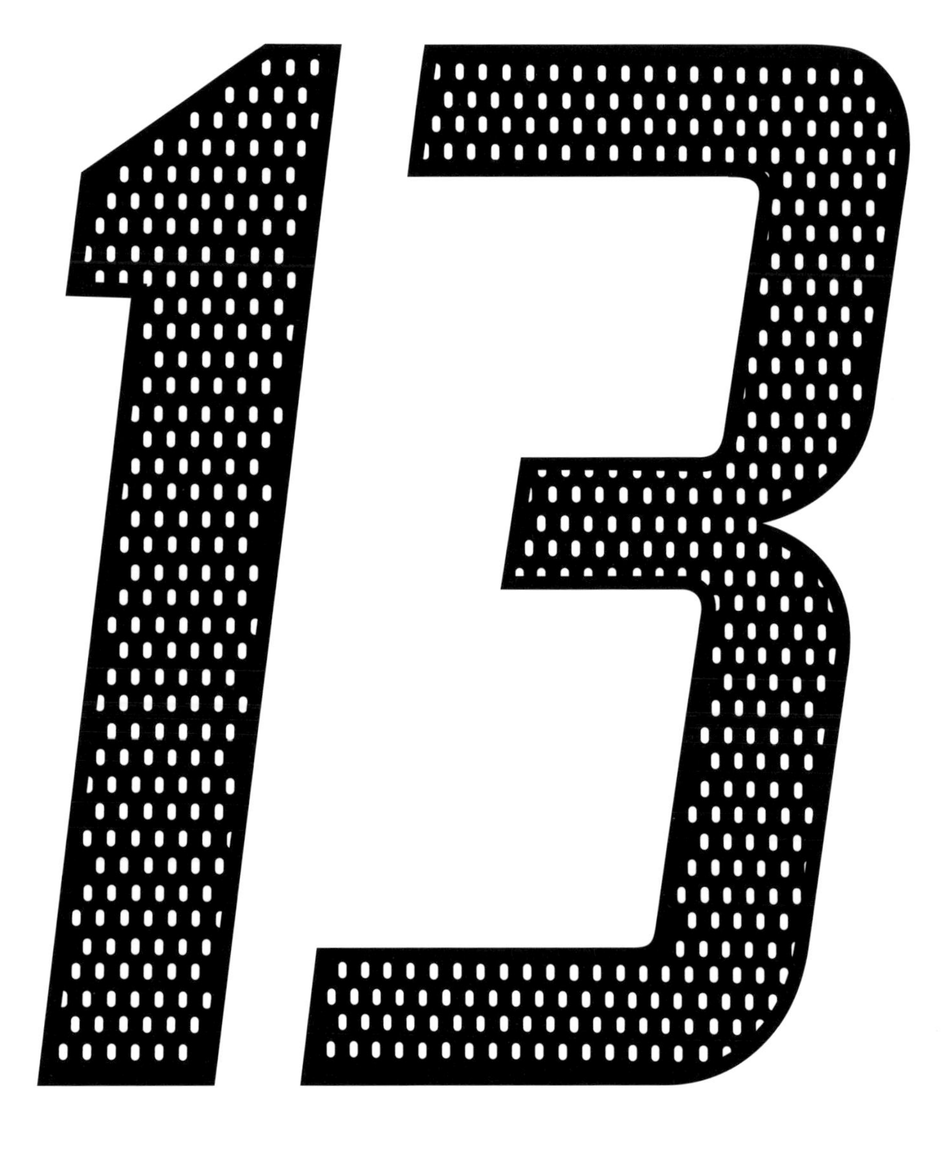
13

Dual-layered shirts, designed to aid ventilation, were *en vogue* with adidas and Nike for the 2002 World Cup in Japan and South Korea.

The German firm carried the principle through to their numbering as well, with perforations throughout, apart from a solid outline. This was a modified version of Serpentine and was a big change from the style of the 1990s.

Country
Germany

Typeface
Serpentine (distorted)

Year
2002

Photography
mooneyphoto

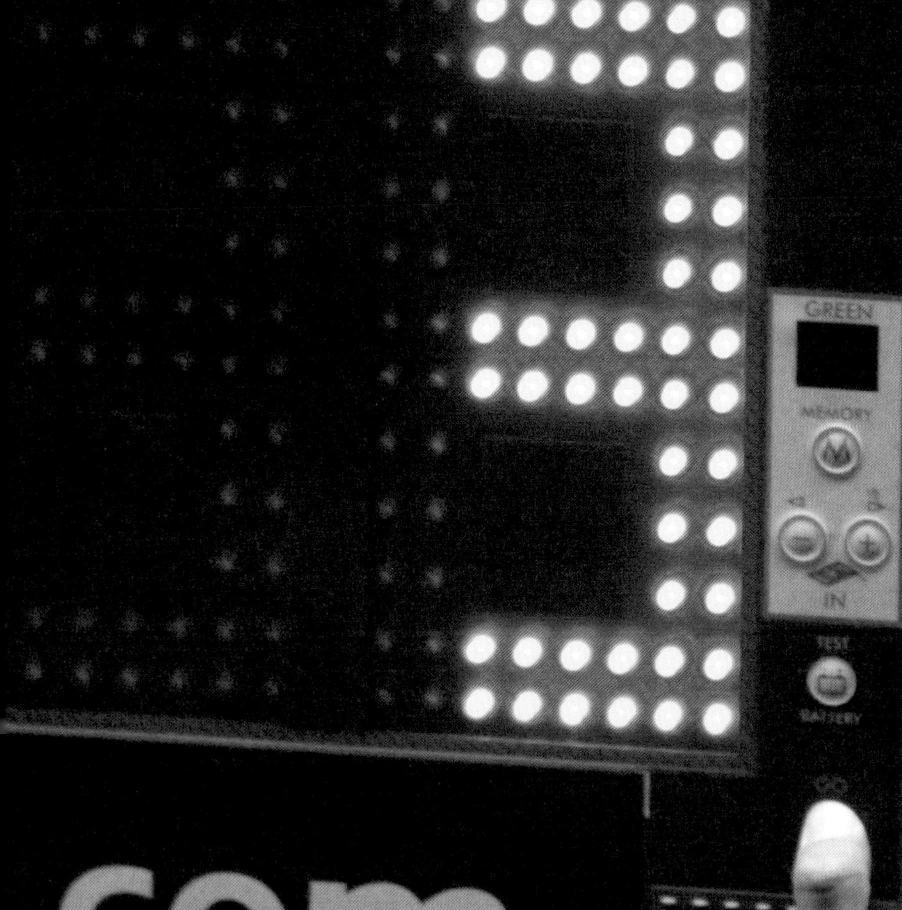
GREEN
MEMORY
IN
.com

In keeping with the philosophy of creating a holistic, overarching 'brand', 2002 saw the introduction of a bespoke typeface for the Football Association. This was designed by typographer Jeremy Tankard under the direction of design studio Elmwood.

This was intended to be used in all FA communications so as to create a letter-form so distinctive that it was immediately identifiable as 'England'.

Two years later, Sporting iD came up with a stretched version of the typeface for the new England away kit designed for Euro 2004.

Country
England

Typeface
FA Caps (distorted)

Year
2004

Design
Sporting iD

12345
67890
ABCcDEFGHI
JKLMNOPQR
STUVWXYZ.

BECKHAM
7

Photography
mooneyphoto

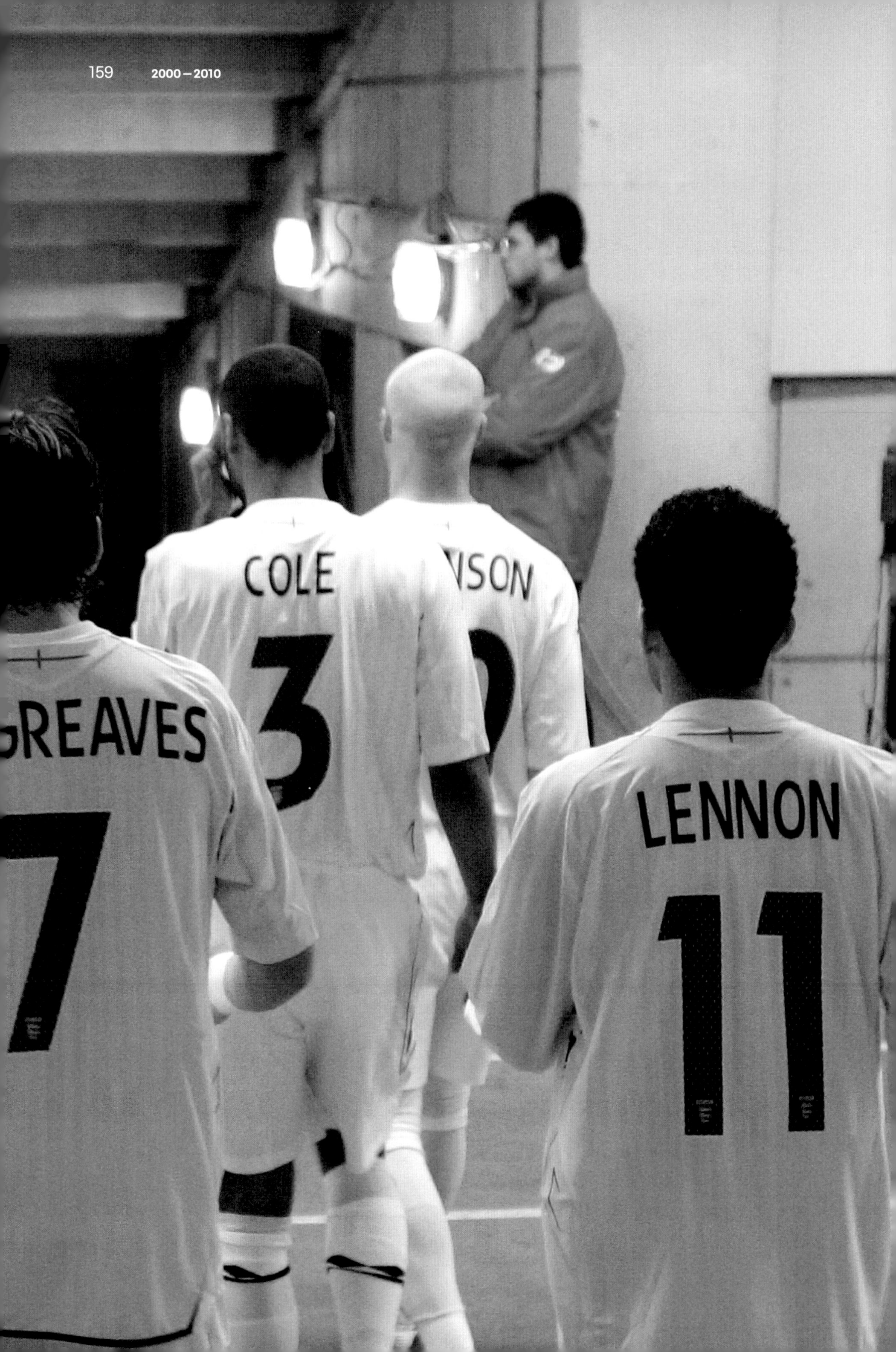
COLE
3
GREAVES
7
LENNON
11

Like everything, design goes through phases – compare this Umbro Nº 8 with that of Fabio Capello from 1974 [p63]. The Republic of Ireland didn't launch a new home shirt for the 2002 World Cup but the slab-serif font used during qualifying was replaced with this new typeface, which Chelsea also used in European competition from 2002-03 onwards. A notable feature was the Nº 3, which was a mirror-image of the set's 'E'.

Club
Chelsea F.C.

Typeface
Custom

Year
2005

Design
Umbro

1234567890

ABCcDEFGHIJKLMNOPQRSTUVWWXYZ

LAMPARD

Constructed over the period 1989-1996, Madrid's KIO Towers (named after the Kuwait Investment Office, which commissioned them) are 115m tall with an inclination of 15 degrees, making them the first inclined skyscrapers in the world.

The Towers' nickname, the Gateway to Europe, reference Real Madrid's success in the European Cup and Champions League and so it made sense that they would form the basis for a typeface for the club.

For 2005-06, Los Merengues' shirts carried this Anthony Barnett design, which italicised and coloured the tall font Peignot in order to imitate the famous buildings.

Club
Real Madrid C.F.

Typeface
Peignot (distorted)

Year
2005

Design
Sporting iD

Designer
Anthony Barnett

123456
7890
abcçdefghijklm
ñopqrstuvwxyz

Club
FC Bayern Munich

Typeface
Industria

Year
2005

French left-back Bixente Lizarazu joined Bayern Munich from Athletic Bilbao in 1997 (his Basque roots entitled him to play for Los Rojiblancos).

Having worn Nº 11 in his first season in Bavaria, he switched to the more fitting Nº 3 when it became free the following year and held that until the end of 2004-05, when he joined Olympique Marseille.

He wore Nº 3 in France but his stay there only lasted six months and he rejoined Bayern. While he had been away, Brazilian defender Lucio had taken Nº 3 and so Lizarazu opted for Nº 69.

Though it might have been seen as juvenile, the France international pointed out that he was born in 1969, was 1.69m tall and weighed 69kg.

For the final 13 years of his career, French striker Nicolas Anelka wore Nº 39 for seven clubs, with the only exception being the Nº 18 he wore at Juventus in 2012-13.

Having worn Nº 9 for Arsenal, Paris St-Germain and Liverpool, and Nº 19 for Real Madrid, when he joined Manchester City in 2002 he found both of those numbers taken, by Paulo Wanchope and Danny Tiatto respectively, while Shaun Wright-Phillips was in Nº 29.

As a result, he opted for Nº 39 and that became his number, including for his three-year spell at Fenerbahçe from 2004-07. The Istanbul club's font, design by Anthony Barnett for Sporting iD, was based on waving flags and included Turkish accents.

Club
Fenerbahçe S.K.

Typeface
Custom

Year
2005

Design
Sporting iD

Designer
Anthony Barnett

Photography
Mat Wright

When Mexican attacker Adolfo 'Bo-fo' Bautista wore Nº 99 for CD Guadalajara, or 'Chivas', in 2005, it might have been expected that that was as high as he would go.

However, three digits are not uncommon in Mexico, with clubs giving every player in their system a unique number and so Bofo opted to wear Nº 100 in 2006. Soon after that, he transferred to Jaguares de Chiapas and went for the other extreme, wearing Nº 1.

While he donned Nº 7 when he returned to Chivas a few years later and wore Nº 10 for other clubs, his farewell game in 2017 saw Bofo and all of his team-mates wearing Nº 100.

Club
Club Deportivo Guadalajara 'Chivas'

Typeface
Custom

Year
2005

Design
Reebok

"Big-name striker completes signing" was a headline that followed Jan Vennegoor of Hesselink throughout a career that took in FC Twente, PSV (twice), Celtic, Hull City and Rapid Vienna.

The Dutch international's unusual moniker dated from the 17th century, when two noble families in Enschede (where Twente are based), the Vennegoors and the Hesselinks, were joined in marriage.

As the two names were of equal prestige, they were combined — 'of' means 'or' in Dutch. When Jan joined Hull in 2009-10, initially his name arched over the entire number, as with the Celtic example below, but the Tigers later opted for narrower letters, as also used on Shaun Wright-Phillips' Chelsea shirt at the time.

Club
Celtic F.C.

Typefaces
Futura (Names, distorted) &
Eras (Numbers)

Year
2006

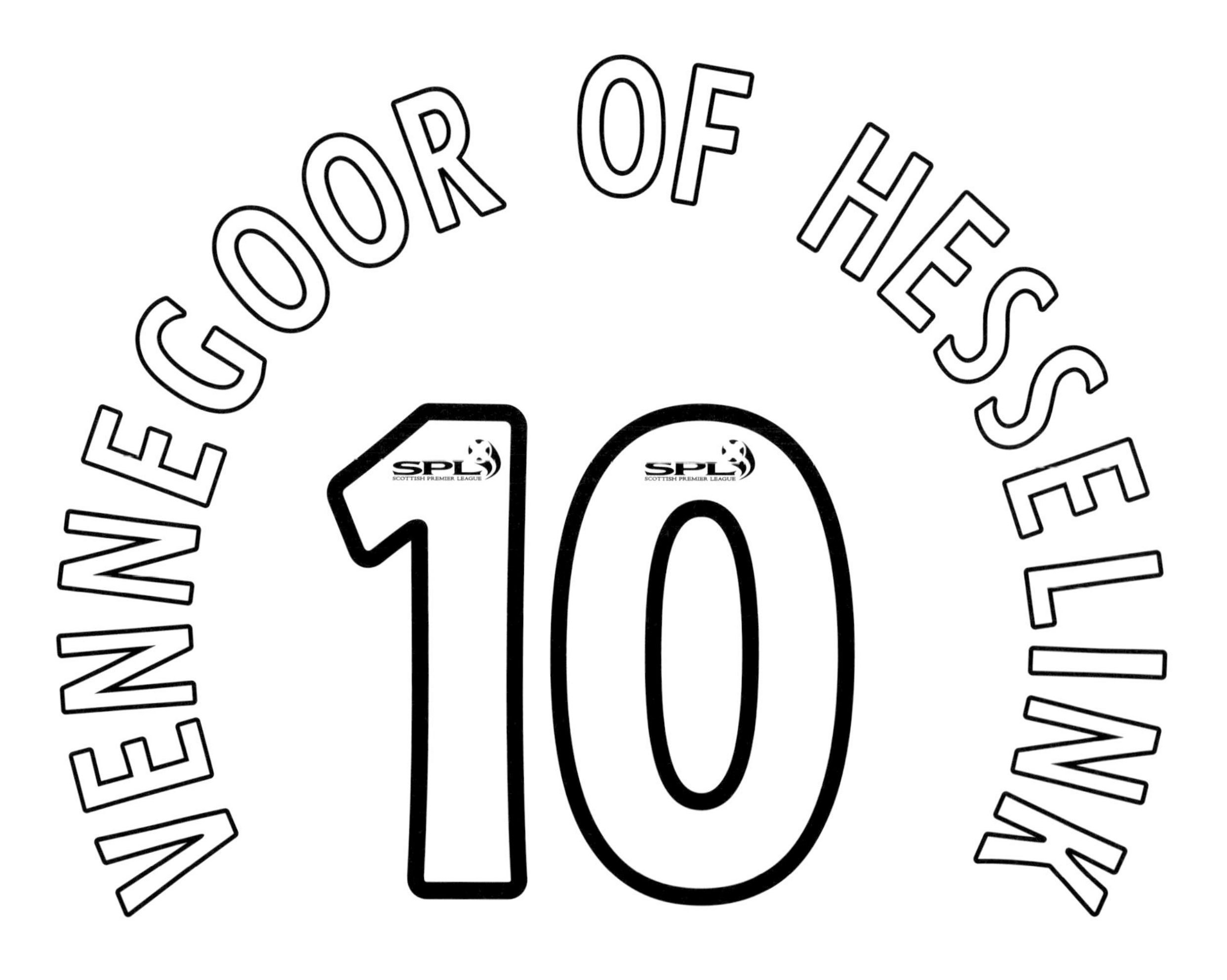

While Hicham Zerouali's time with Aberdeen was short, he left his mark.

The Moroccan, who would tragically die in a car accident in 2004, joined the Dons from FUS de Rabat for £450,000 in November 1999. With Aberdeen having a full roster, he was given the lowest number available, 47, and made an immediate impact.

The Aberdeen fans adopted him as a cult-hero, and for his first full season, 'Zero' decided to live up to his nickname by switching to Nº 0. A bad ankle injury, which ruled him out of the Olympic Games in Sydney, limited him to just seven appearances in that 2000-01 season.

For 2001-02, the Scottish Premier League had changed the results so that Nº 1 was the lowest that could be used and Zero opted for Nº 11.

Club
Aberdeen F.C.

Typefaces
Futura (Names, distorted) &
Eras (Numbers)

Year
2000

TO DARE IS TO DO

TOTTENHAM
HOTSPUR™

One of the most successful overall branding exercises of recent times was Tottenham Hotspur's in 2006.

There was certainly a risk involved for a club with a heritage like Tottenham's, with a fanbase spanning generations and numbering millions worldwide. To get a rebranding wrong would be to run the possibility of alienating those supporters.

Edinburgh company Navy Blue were — fittingly — chosen to refresh the Spurs identity and, interestingly, to 'soften' it so as to increase its appeal to female fans.

While the 'Audere est Facere' crest introduced in the 1980s held a fond place in the hearts of many Spurs fans, elements such as the 'THFC' monogram and the lions rampant were considered disposable. The famous cockerel on a football was naturally non-negotiable but it was reworked by navy blue, harking back to the club's classic crest, as used when they won the domestic double in 1961.

In addition, Dalton Maag created a typeface, simply called 'Spurs', for use on practically everything associated with the club, ensuring that kits, communications, merchandise and signage are tied together in a consistent and vibrant fashion.

Such has been the success of this font, that, 13 years later it is still being used today.

Club
Tottenham Hotspur F.C.

Typeface
Spurs

Year
2006

Design
Navy Blue

Type Designer
Bruno Maag

- . / 0 1 2
3 4 5 6 7 8
9 @ A B C D
E F G H I J
K L M N O P
Q R S T U V
W X Y Z

Club & Countries
Names & numbers
for all PUMA teams

Typeface
PUMA Pace

Year
2006

Design
GBH

Font developer
Bruno Maag

An all-lowercase letterset may not seem too out of the ordinary now, but back in 2006 it was certainly noteworthy. While FIFA stipulate position and size regulations, there are no demands regarding case.

Design studio GBH were commissioned by PUMA to design a font for the World Cup in Germany that year and 'Pace' was what resulted, intended to reinforce the PUMA brand.

Type designer Bruno Maag, who digitised 'Pace', explains the background to create such a look: "The basis was sketches, developed from a rectangle, without integrated curves."

"We worked on different versions of the serifs, but in the end decided the original was the best."

Rapidity was the theme, with the italic slant and the 'wind tunnel' speed lines intended to represent speed. Guidelines on positioning and kerning were created by Sporting iD for PUMA.

Italy, with gold 'Pace' detailing on their kits, won the World Cup, ensuring the widest possible exposure for the names and numbers.

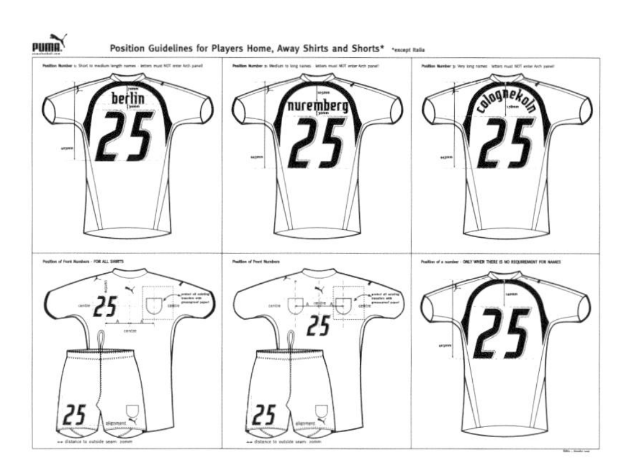

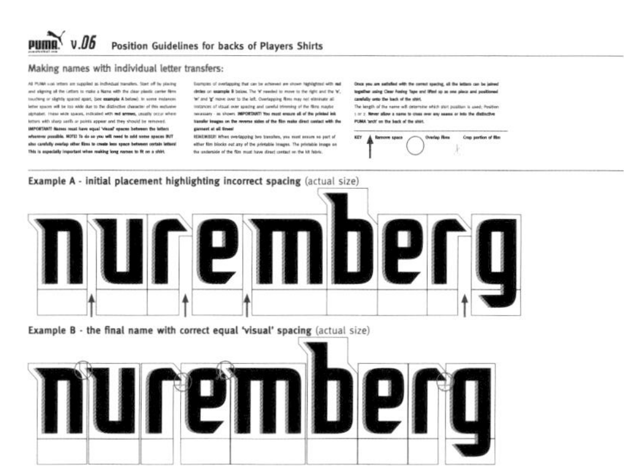

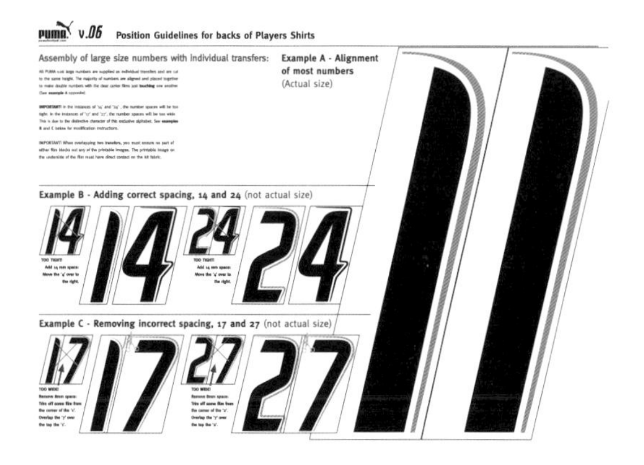

Squad numbers were introduced in Serie A in 1995-96. In that first season, Parma gave teenage goalkeeper Gianluigi Buffon the Nº 12 shirt and, two years later, he graduated to the Nº 1.

However, while his status wasn't in doubt, the custodian fancied a change for 2000-01 and announced that he would wear Nº 88. Immediately, there was outcry from Italy's Jewish community.

Buffon, who had previously worn a shirt with the slogan 'Boia chi molla', or 'Death to cowards', which was used by fascists in the Benito Mussolini era, was accused of being a Neo-Nazi as 'H' is the eighth letter of the alphabet and 88 is often used to indicate 'HH' or 'Heil Hitler'.

The goalkeeper insisted that that was not the reason and instead put it down to a desire to win back his national team place after injury caused him to miss Euro 2000. "I have chosen 88 because it reminds me of four balls. In Italy, we all know what it means to have balls: strength and determination. I'll need balls to win back my place in the Italy side."

However, in order to avoid further controversy, he wore Nº 77 in what would be his final season with Parma. He joined Juventus in 2001 and wore Nº 1 in Turin for 17 seasons before he joined Paris Saint-Germain. After just a season in France, he returned to Juventus in the summer of 2019 and, with Wojciech Szczęsny now wearing Nº 1 for Juventus, Buffon opted for Nº 77 again.

buffon

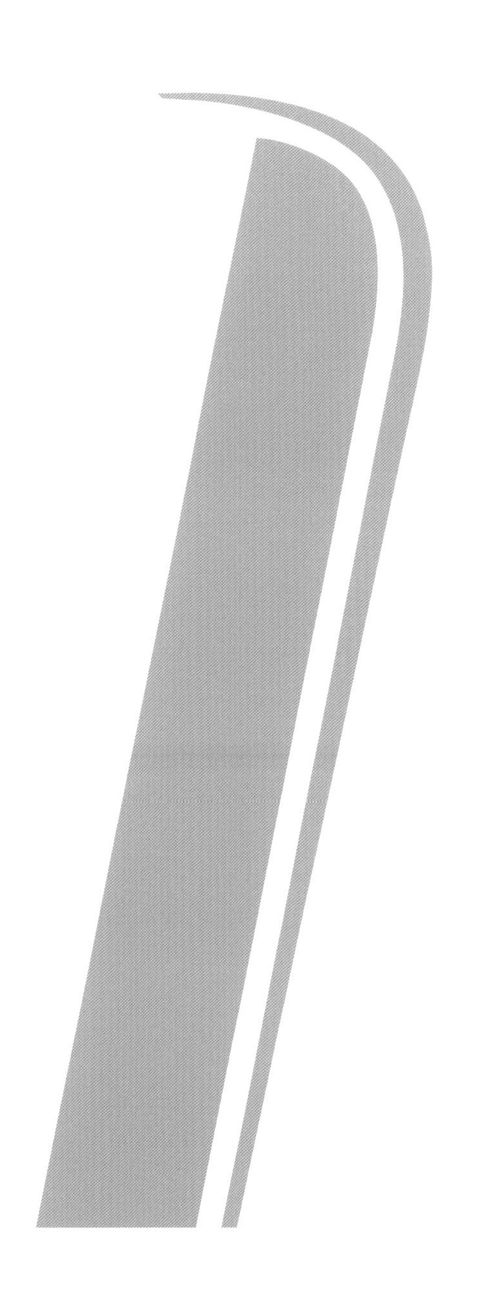

Past and present influences were at play in the adidas font for the 2006 World Cup in the company's native Germany.

The echo lines of the 'Teamgeist', the official match ball for the World Cup, were an inspiration as well as the iconic three-stripe numbering first seen in the 1970s [p56].

A modern twist was provided as the digits were made up of four stripes, though the narrower gaps between them did form three-stripe patterns.

Countries
Names & numbers
for all adidas teams

Typeface
ITC Bauhaus (Names)
& Custom (Numbers)

Year
2006

Design
Dekographics

0
2
1
3
4
5
6
7
8
9

BRASIL
RONALDO
9

Local influences for the global stage were the driving force for Nike's number fonts at the 2006 World Cup.

The design team travelled extensively to come up with unique cultural inspirations for each top-tier team, produced in collaboration with type foundry MADtype.

A font called 'Nameplate' was used for the names while the numbers from that set were used by second-tier nations and carried forward for club teams the following season.

Club & Countries
Names & numbers for all Nike teams

Typeface
Nameplate (Names) & Custom (Numbers)

Year
2006

Creative Director, Nike
Heather Amuny-Dey

Designers, Nike
Adam Cohn, Julie Freeman & Remco Vloon

Design
MADType

Type Designer
Matthew Desmond

Photography
Carlos Serrao

Nameplate

ABCDEFGHIJKLMN
OPQRSTUVWXYZ
abcdefghijklmn
opqrstuvwxyz

BRASIL

0123456789

NEDERLAND

0123456789

MEXICO

0123456789

РОССИЯ

0123456789

PORTUGAL

0123456789

TÜRKIYE

0123456789

MAROC

0123456789

KOREA

0123456789

USA

0123456789

Tier 2

0123456789

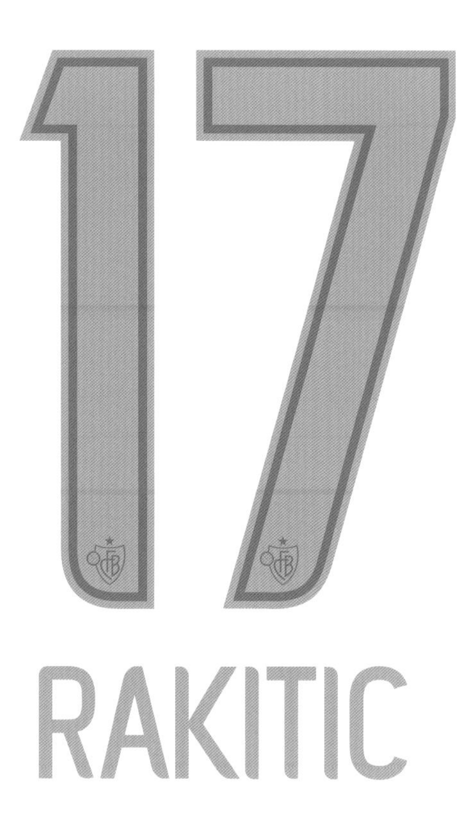

Club
Inter Milan

Typeface
Custom

Year
2007

Club
FC Basel

Typeface
Nameplate

Year
2007

Design
MADType

Designer
Matthew Desmond

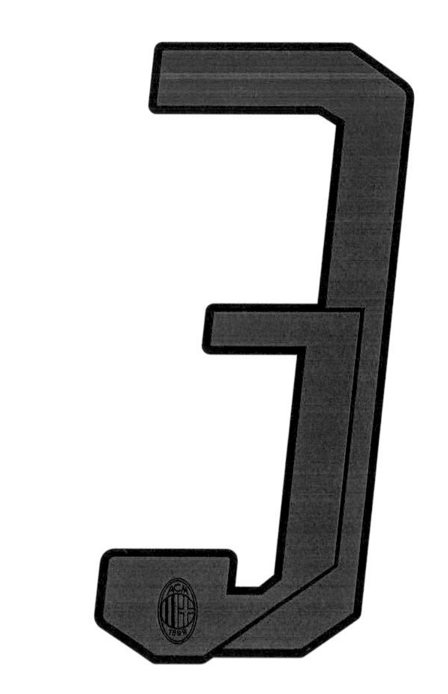

Club
A.C. Milan

Typeface
Custom

Year
2007

MATERAZZI

23

ROONEY
10
MANCHESTER UNITED
MANCHESTER UNITED

This unique font, with concave shapes inside convex 'frames', was designed by Sporting iD for Manchester United in consultation with Nike, with United manager Sir Alex Ferguson having the final say.

It appeared in Europe during 2007-08, including the famous Champions League final win over Chelsea in Moscow, but United used the normal Premier League font for domestic cup competitions.

While the United home shirt launched in 2007 was the last to have a two-year lifespan, a simpler numbering style was used for the Champions League in 2008-09.

Club
Manchester United F.C.

Typeface
Custom

Year
2007

Design
Sporting iD

Designer
Anthony Barnett

From the moment Zinedine Zidane swung his boot at the ball to volley Real Madrid to victory against Bayer Leverkusen to secure a ninth European title in 2002, thoughts turned to La Décima or a tenth.

For 2007-08, Sporting iD created a font based around this quest, with the ten-sided decagon shape forming the basis for the numbers.

The look was striking and, while European glory would remain elusive until 2014 – the first of four Champions Leagues in five years – they impressed domestically, with a 31st league title claimed.

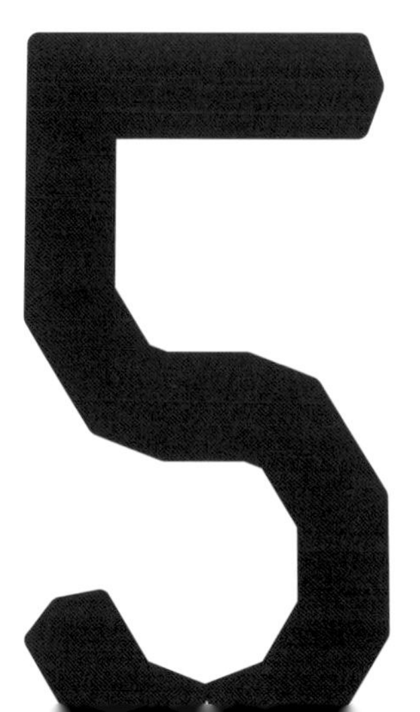

Club
Real Madrid C.F.

Typeface
Custom

Year
2007

Design
Sporting iD

Designer
Anthony Barnett

Club & Countries
Names & numbers
for all PUMA teams

Typeface
PUMA Pixel

Year
2007

Design
PUMA

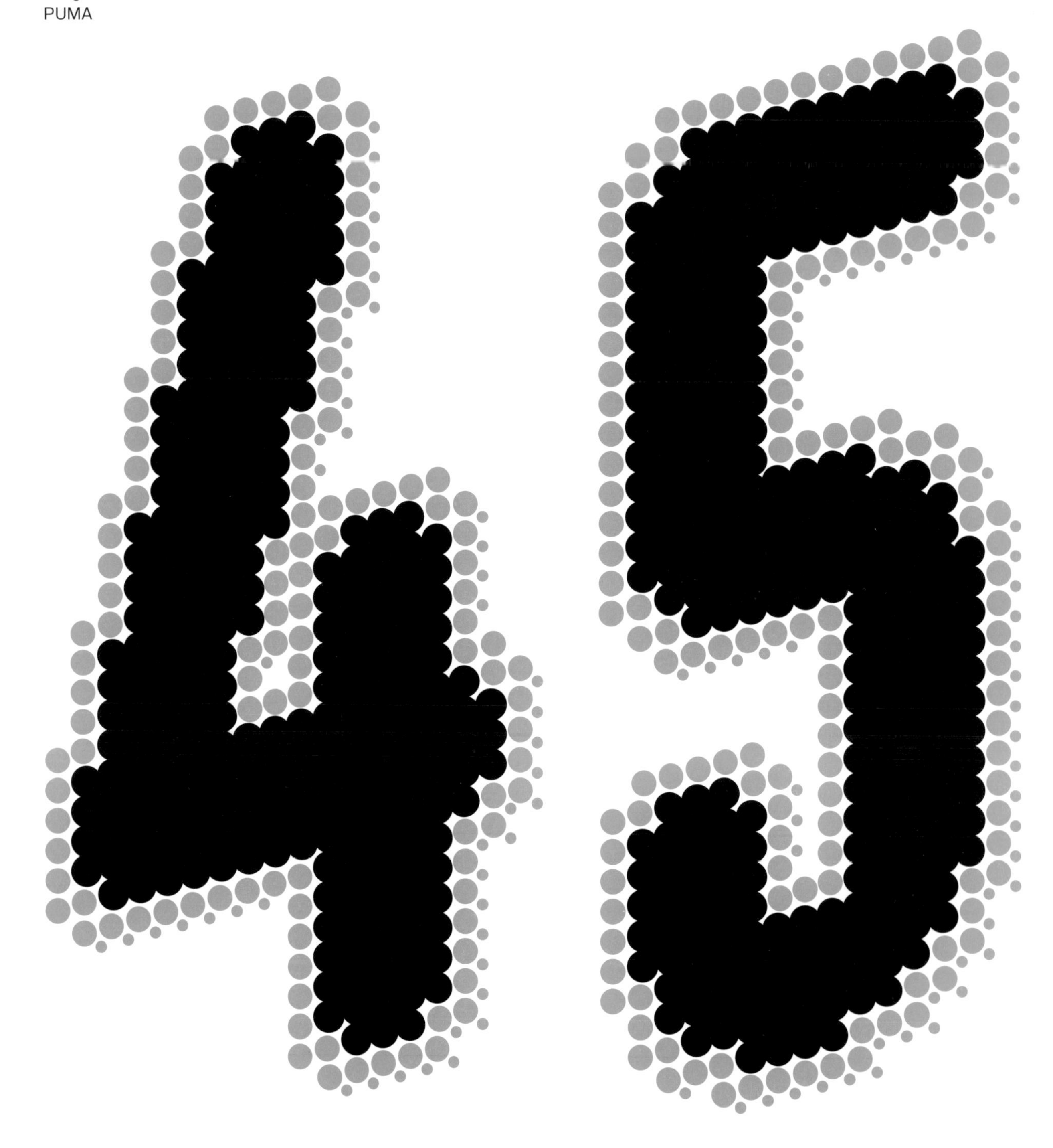

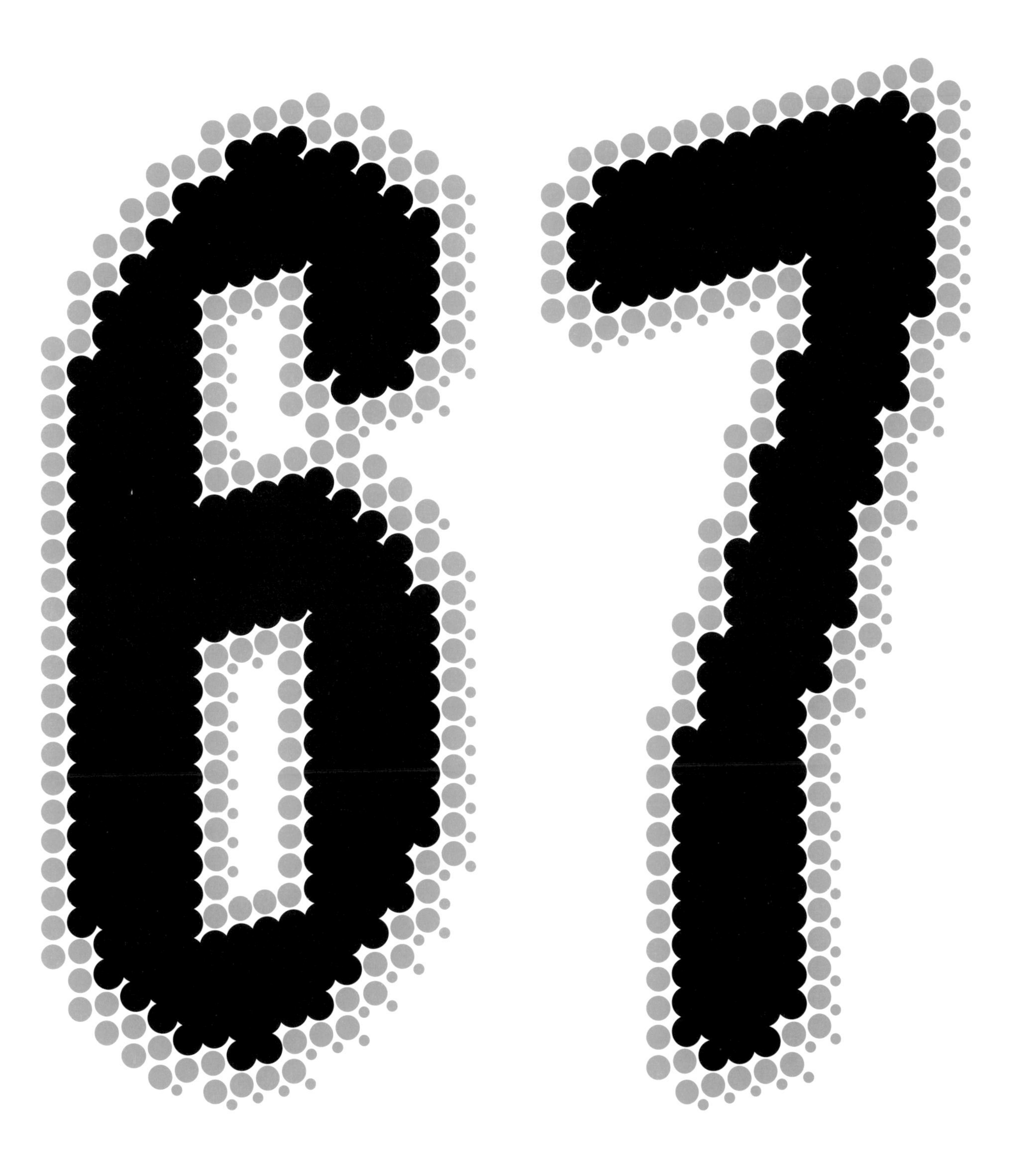

GIGGS
11

There were changes afoot in 2007 as the 'FA' was dropped from the Premier League title, while the decision was made not to have a title sponsor so as to promote the strength of the brand.

Visually, there were differences too as, for the first time since the introduction of a uniform numbering style in 2007, a new font was unveiled.

Designed by Sporting iD, the new typeface was intended to improve player identification for those watching in stadiums or on television. In addition, it featured on all Premier League communications.

Ryan Giggs was the only player to wear the Manchester United Nº 11 in the Premier League from the introduction of squad numbers in 1993 until his retirement in 2014.

While the number was allocated to Adnan Januzaj for the following season, he only held it for two years before it was taken by Anthony Martial as he switched from Nº 9 to allow Zlatan Ibrahimović to wear it.

Brand
Premier League

Typeface
Premier League

Year
2007

Design
Sporting iD

APPLICATION GUIDE

ALPHABET

ABCDEFGHIJ
KLMNOQRSTU
VWXYZ ĆV̆ , . -

NUMBERS

1234567890

COLOURS

PLAYER 12 PLAYER 12 PLAYER 12 PLAYER 12 PLAYER 12

POSITIONING

"Play for the name on the front and they'll remember the name on the back" — David Bentley might have hoped that that wasn't the case in this shirt.

Elongate the final letter of Sergio Agüero's name and most football fans will get the reference — Manchester City supporters certainly will, after the way in why Sky commentator Martin Tyler greeted the Premier League-winning goal on the final day of the 2011-12 season.

That season had seen Mario Balotelli celebrate a goal in the 6-1 win over Manchester United at Old Trafford by revealing a t-shirt with the 'Why always me?' slogan. If you're thinking that the Premier League letterset didn't include a question-mark, you'd be right — kitman Les Chapman re-engineered a 'P' with scissors.

Balotelli wore Nº 45 during his time at City as, when he was a youngster at Inter Milan, youths were given between Nº 36 and Nº 50, so he opted for 45 as four and five added up to nine. He also wore Nº 45 at AC Milan and Liverpool but when he joined OGC Nice in 2016, league rules limited players to numbers no higher than 30 and so he opted for Nº 9, later wearing it for Olympique Marseille.

Photography
Carl Recine

Photography
Kieran McManus

Photography
Sam Bagnall | AMA

Club
UPB-MyTeam FC

Typeface
ITC Neon

Year
2007

In 2006, a Malaysian reality TV show called *MyTeam* brought together a group of players from across the country with no professional experience, charting their progress before leading to a gala match against the national team.

After a 2-1 defeat, politician Khairy Jamaluddin and radio DJ Jason Lo — the co-creator of *MyTeam* — took over ailing side UPB FC and re-named it UPBMyTeam. They finished second in the Malaysian Premier League in 2007, earning promotion to the Super League for the following season. However, the team was dissolved in 2009.

Country
England

Typeface
Custom

Year
2008

Club
FC Shakhtar Donetsk

Typeface
Aurora (distorted)

Year
2008

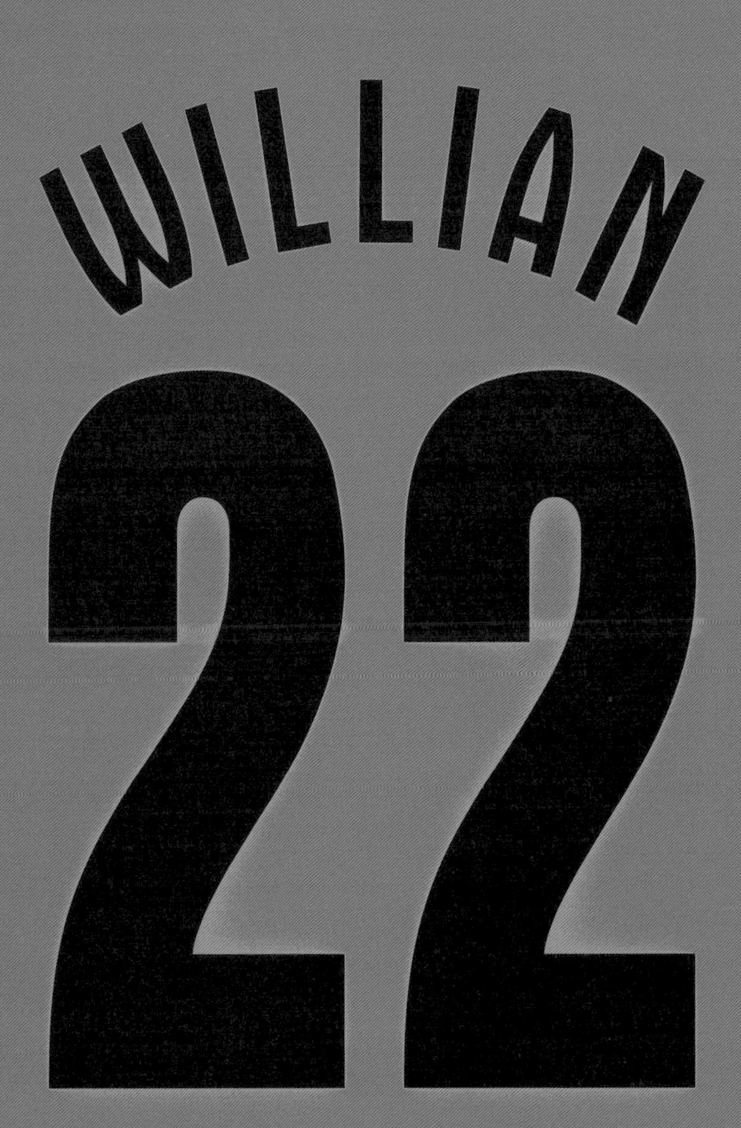

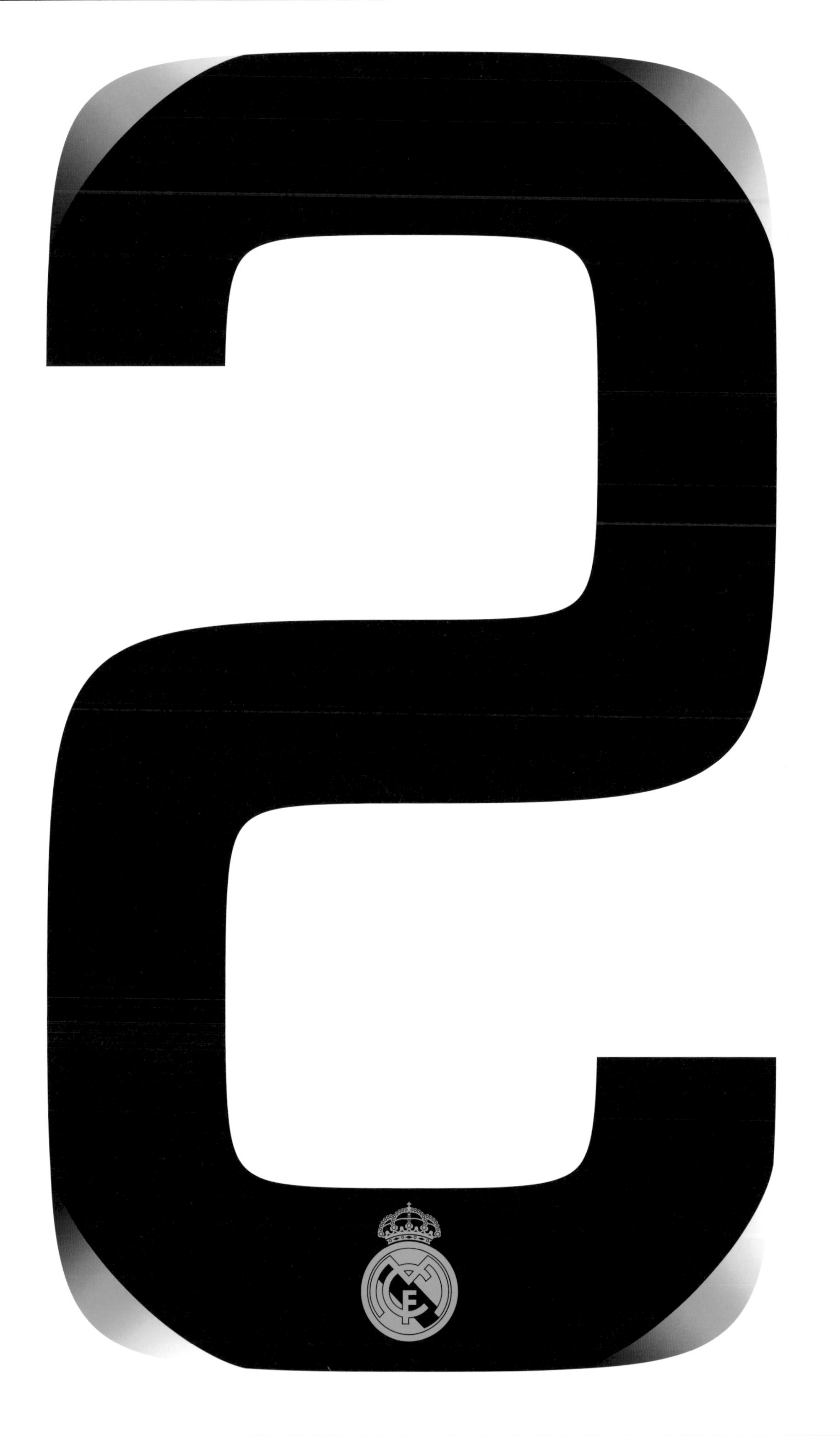

The 2007-08 season marked the 60th anniversary of the completion of Real Madrid's Estadio Santiago Bernabéu.

This special occasion was the basis for the club's numbering for that campaign, with Sporting iD creating a set which referenced the shape of the stadium.

Club
Real Madrid C.F.

Typeface
Custom

Year
2008

Design
Sporting iD

Designer
Anthony Barnett

PUMA had two fonts on show at Euro 2008. The pixel style introduced the previous year [p192] was on the first-choice kits of joint-hosts Austria, the Czech Republic, Italy, Poland and Switzerland. Then, a new typeface, which featured vertical lines 'cutting' through the numbers and lowercase letters, was on the five countries' change strips.

Unfortunately, it wasn't a tournament to remember for the firm as Italy were the only one of the quintet to make it to the knockout stages, losing to Spain on penalties in the quarter-finals.

Club & Countries
Names & numbers for all PUMA teams

Typeface
Euro Championship

Year
2008

Design
PUMA

abcdefghijklm
nopqrstuvwxy

0123456789

While the Spanish (1-25) and French (1-30) leagues are strict on which numbers can be worn, there are no such regulations in Italy and, soon after squad numbers were introduced in Serie A in 1995, high digits soon became common.

A popular trope was for players to wear their birth years on their backs and this was very apparent at AC Milan in 2008-09.

Among The Rossoneri's signings were Ronaldinho from Barcelona, Mathieu Flamini from Arsenal and Andriy Shevchenko, back from Chelsea. Ronaldinho had worn 10 at Barça and Paris Saint-Germain before, with Flamini 16 for the Gunners while Shevchenko wore 7 at Stamford Bridge and also in his first spell with Milan, but those numbers were taken by Clarence Seedorf, Željko Kalac and Alexandre Pato respectively.

The solution for the trio was to show their ages by donning their birth years — 80 for Ronaldinho, 84 for Flamini and 76 for Shevchenko.

Club
A.C. Milan

Typeface
Custom

Year
2008

In keeping with the philosophy of having a theme across all of its output for a single tournament, adidas applied a consistent approach for Euro 2008.

Curved and rounded lines were common on their kits and the official match ball, the Europass, and the same approach was taken with the names and numbers set, which had soft corners to give a fluid, dynamic feel.

Countries
Names & numbers for all adidas teams

Typeface
adidas Euro 2008

Year
2008

Design
adidas

Senior Design Director, adidas
Jürgen Rank

1234567890

ABCDEFGHIJKLMNOPQRSTUVWXYZ

STELIOS

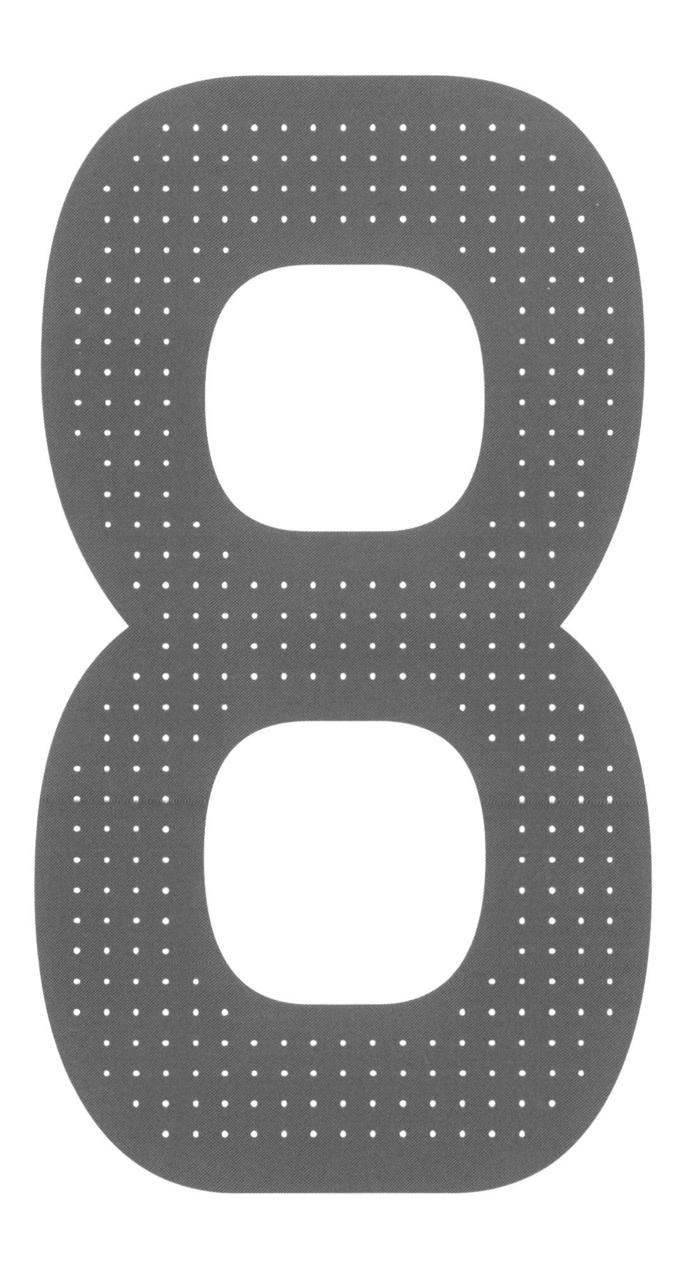

While Cristiano Ronaldo had made the famous Manchester United Nº 7 his own, upon his transfer to Real Madrid in 2009 he had to take Nº 9.

Club legend Raúl held Nº 7 and, similar to how, in 2001, Zinedine Zidane had to opt for Nº 5 as Luís Figo had Nº 10, Ronaldo was forced to choose a different number for his first season in the Spanish capital. Raúl joined Schalke 04 in 2010, freeing up Nº 7 for Ronaldo.

Real's 2009-10 font, created by Sporting iD, had a unique 3D effect, created by a pearlescent pattern. Given the popularity of Ronaldo and the global reach of the Real fanbase, replica shirts were made available with his name rendered in the Chinese, Japanese and Arabic alphabets.

Club
Real Madrid C.F.

Typeface
Custom

Year
2009

Design
Sporting iD

Designer
Anthony Barnett

ABCDEFGH
IJKLMNOP
QRSTUVW
XYZ-.,c
1234567890

Dismissed by some as 'just a polo shirt', Umbro's England 2009 kit was so much more, combining the traditional values of bespoke tailoring with modern fabric technology.

The accompanying letters and numbers were designed by Sporting iD, who took the 1966 style [p31] as a starting point.

The 1960s stitching style was imitated with the inclusion of a 3D effect, while the laser-cut, perforated material was affixed with a minimum-contact bonding system. This lightweight heat transfer created a pocket which allowed the cloth within the numbers to breathe.

Country
England

Typeface
Custom

Year
2009

Design
Sporting iD

TERRY
6

(25mm)
6
(70mm)
TERRY
(55mm)
6
6
(15mm)
JAMES
1
1

To tie in with the 'Tailored by' approach of the kit-design, in 2010 Umbro painted a wall in the home town of each member of England's World Cup squad. Each wall featured the player's squad number and the famous 'Tailored by', followed by the placename.

As well as the 23 players' native homes, Umbro also decorated a wall in San Canzian d'Isonzo in Italy, the birthplace of manager Fabio Capello.

Number 5
Rio Ferdinand

Number 9
Peter Crouch

Number 20
Ledley King

TOTTI

10

Club
A.S. Roma

Typeface
Whitman Display (distorted)

Year
2009

Club
FC Schalke 04

Typeface
ITC Grizzly

Year
2009

Club
Malmö FF

Typeface
Harry

Year
2009

2010
2020

For the 2010 World Cup in South Africa, adidas once again linked the official match ball – the Jabulani – with its font, which was known as ‘UNITY’.

The Jabulani featured a central delta-shaped panel, signifying the ‘heart’ of the World Cup, and Unity drew upon that shape with its numbering and lettering.

As well as on the shirts for: Argentina, Denmark, Paraguay, France, Japan, Germany, Slovakia, Mexico, Nigeria, Greece, South Africa and Spain, Unity was on the packaging of all adidas World Cup products and of course the Jabulani.

An audience of millions was exposed to Unity as it featured in every adidas World Cup communication and in film, content, print, digital, gaming and events.

!"#$%&'()*+,-./0123456789:;
<=>?@ABCDEFGHIJKLMNOPQ
RSTUVXYZ[\]^_`aabcdeffifl
ghijklmnopqrstuvwxyz{|}¡¢£
¥¦§¨©ª«¬®°±´µ¶·¸º»¿ÀÁÂÃÄ
ÅÆÇÈÉÊËÌÍÎÏÐÑÒÓÔÕÖØÙÚÛÜ
Ýàáâãäåæçèéêëìíîïðñòóôõö
÷øùúûüýþÿĂăČıŁłŒœŠšŸŽž
ˆˇ˘˙˚˛˜˝;ΑΕΚΛΟΠΡΣΥΩάαδλοπ
ρςύЇЈАДДЕИКМНОРСУЯадде
икнорсяј–—‘’“”†‡•…‰‹›/€™Δ

Countries
Names & numbers for all adidas teams

Typeface
UNITY

Year
2010

Design
adidas

Senior Design Director, adidas
Jürgen Rank

MESSI 10
BALLACK 13
CASILLAS 1

ARH
357

APPIAH

10

Paul Barnes of Commercial Type designed the font for the African teams with PUMA contracts competing in the 2010 Africa Cup of Nations and the World Cup.

The aim for Barnes was to incorporate a hand-made feel, with elements of a brush-stroke. The use of body paints by fans who wrote their favourite players' names on their flesh was an inspiration, with the intention to express a natural joy and exuberance.

Countries
Names & numbers for African PUMA teams

Typeface
Darren

Year
2010

Design
Commercial Type

Designer
Paul Barnes

1234567890
ABCDEFGHIJKLMNOPQRSTUVWXYZ
abcdefghijklmnopqrstuvwxyz
{(["£$&€!?@%"])}

For the 2010 World Cup, a separate font was created by Paul Barnes for PUMA's non-African teams.

The primary aim for this typeface was to blend simple geometric lettering traditionally related to sport with no-nonsense technical forms.

"The numbers have a slightly different feel," Barnes said. "They have the outer forms of a typical grotesque, but the interiors have a geometric feel."

For Italy, names appeared in lower case and sentence case for Uruguay.

A B C D
E F G H
I J K L
M N O P
Q R S T
U V W X
Y Z a b
c d e f
g h i j
k l m n
o p q r
s t u v
w x y z

Countries
Names & numbers for all PUMA teams

Typeface
Crepello

Year
2010

Design
Commercial Type

Designer
Paul Barnes

cannavaro

5

1 *Fernando Muslera*

2 *Diego Lugano*

3 *Diego Godín*

4 *Jorge Fucile*

5 *Walter Gargano*

6 *Mauricio Victorino*

7 *Edinson Cavani*

8 *Sebastián Eguren*

9 *Luis Suárez*

10 *Diego Forlán*

11 *Álvaro Pereira*
12 *Juan Castillo*
13 *Sebastián Abreu*
14 *Nicolás Lodeiro*
15 *Diego Pérez*
16 *Maxi Pereira*
17 *Egidio Arévalo*
18 *Ignacio González*
19 *Andrés Scotti*
20 *Álvaro Fernández*

TOURE YAYA

42

Manchester City's 2010-11 font was a nod to their long relationship with Umbro.

On May 5, 1934, City's club secretary Wilf Wild sent a message to what was then known as Humphreys Bros, thanking them for the "jerseys, knickers, hose, slips and anklets" City had worn in the 2-1 win over Portsmouth in the FA Cup Final the previous week.

As was the custom in the cup back then, both sides had had to change kits due to the colour-clash, with City wearing maroon and Portsmouth in white and black. Umbro came across the telegram in their archives and adapted the 'Typewriter' font for 2010-11 — adding small holes to enable breathability and referencing traditional, hand-sewn, fabric numbers.

Fittingly, City reached the 2011 FA Cup final too, beating Stoke City. For the game, the same font was used but with the numbers in white and featuring the coat of arms of the city of Manchester. This too had a historical influence — City had previously worn the coat of arms instead of their own crest for cup finals, as they were representing the whole city. Prior to adopting their badge, rivals Manchester United used the coat of arms for finals too.

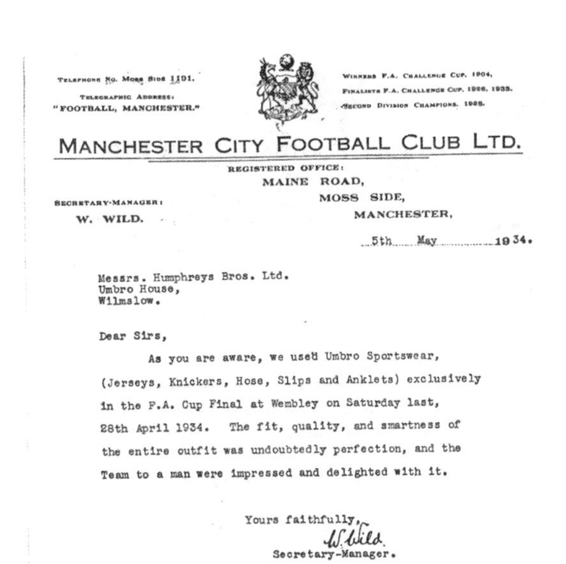

Telephone No. Moss Side 1191.
Telegraphic Address:
"Football, Manchester."

Winners F.A. Challenge Cup. 1904.
Finalists F.A. Challenge Cup. 1926, 1933.
Second Division Champions. 1928.

MANCHESTER CITY FOOTBALL CLUB LTD.

Registered Office:
Maine Road,
Moss Side,
Manchester,

Secretary-Manager:
W. Wild.

5th May 1934.

Messrs. Humphreys Bros. Ltd.
Umbro House,
Wilmslow.

Dear Sirs,

As you are aware, we used Umbro Sportswear, (Jerseys, Knickers, Hose, Slips and Anklets) exclusively in the F.A. Cup Final at Wembley on Saturday last, 28th April 1934. The fit, quality, and smartness of the entire outfit was undoubtedly perfection, and the Team to a man were impressed and delighted with it.

Yours faithfully,
W. Wild.
Secretary-Manager.

Club
Manchester City F.C.

Typeface
Custom

Year
2010

Design
Umbro

ABCDEFGHIJKLMNOPQRSTUVWXYZ
0123456789

Also employing retro influences in 2010-11 were Chelsea. The Blues' kits — including the black and orange change strip — in the Champions League took their cues from the famous 'keyline shadow' introduced by West Germany as they hosted and won the 1974 World Cup [p61].

Club
Chelsea F.C.

Typeface
Custom

Year
2010

Introduced in 2010, this specially-commissioned Liverpool font appeared on the kits of three different manufacturers – adidas, Warrior and New Balance – during its eight-year lifespan.

This serif font had some unique flourishes to ensure it was distinctive and the inclusion of the famous Liver bird ensured that there was unprecedented demand from supporters.

The final game in which the font appeared was the 2018 Champions League final defeat to Real Madrid, with a brand-new style introduced for 2018-19, in which they would go a step further and win the competition for the sixth time [p394].

1

2 6 5 3

7 4 8 11

10 9

Club
Liverpool F.C.

Typeface
LFC European Style

Year
2010

Design
Sporting iD

Designer
Anthony Barnett

GERRARD

CFR Cluj's rise has been meteoric. Prior to an injection of investment in 2002, the club had competed in the Romanian lower leagues, but they won the league for the first time in 2008 and have won four more titles since, including back-to-back wins in 2018 and 2019.

However, their choice of numbers and letters hasn't been without question – this is attacker Saša Bjelanović's shirt from the side's 2010-11 Champions League campaign.

Club
CFR Cluj

Typeface
Park Avenue (distorted)

Year
2011

Lacking the resources to go too bold or brash with their player identification, the Faroe Islands opted to be conservative and chose Times New Roman for their numbering.

Country
Faroe Islands

Typeface
Times New Roman

Year
2011

Even in the normal run of things, the decision of FC Ordabasy from Kazakhstan to employ a 'Wild West' typeface would have been questionable.

To go further and distort it to the point of illegibility ensures its inclusion in the hall of shame.

Club
FC Ordabasy

Typeface
Old Towne Pro (distorted)

Year
2011

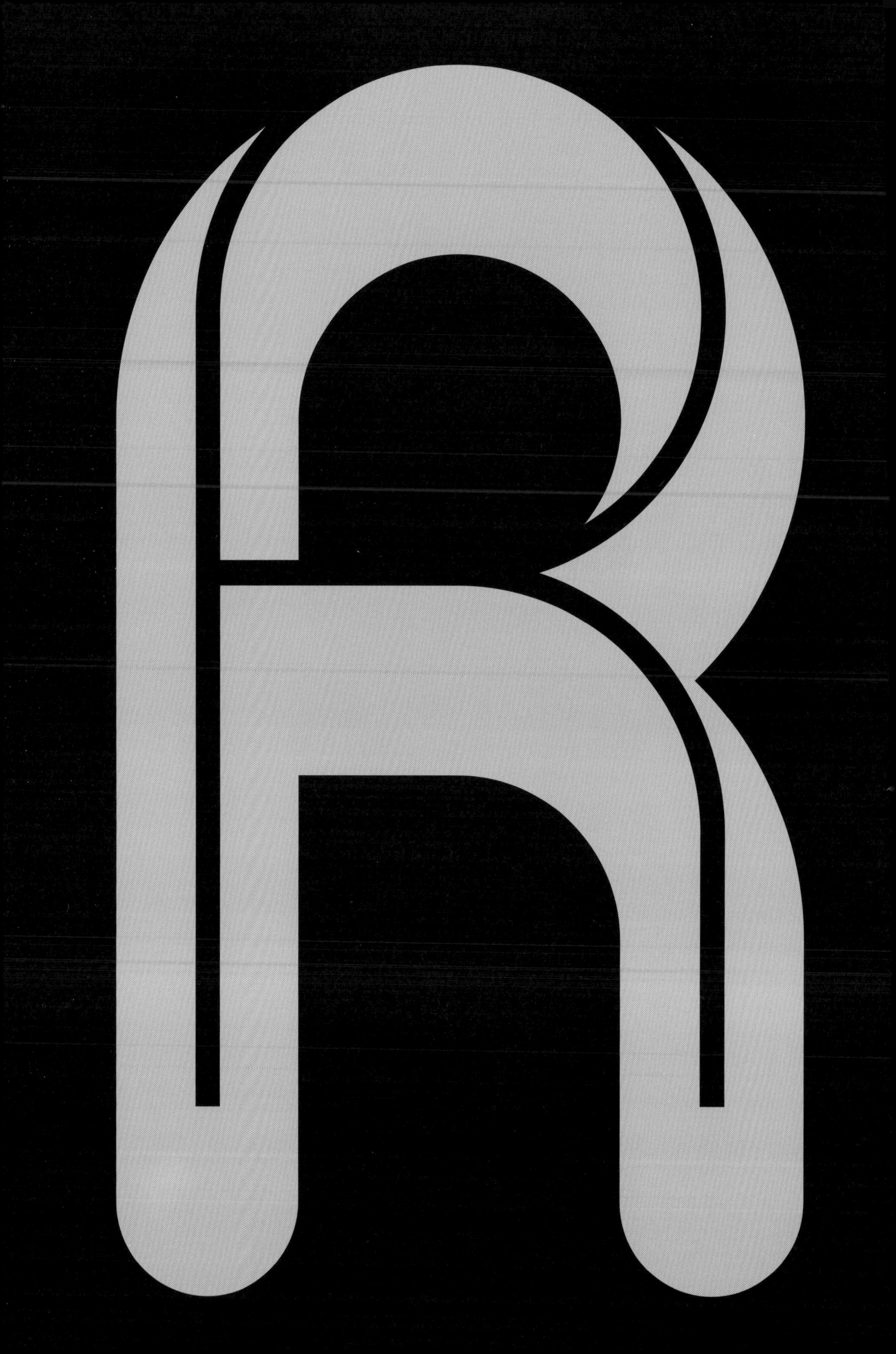

ABCDEFG
HIJKLM
NOPQRST
UVWXYZ

A regal gold was the trim colour for Real Madrid as they ended a four-year wait for the Spanish league title in 2011-12 and Sporting iD came up with numbers and letters to match.

Anthony Barnett designed the optical style, with the line through the figures giving a 'raised' effect. Inspiration from the club's (pardon the pun) golden era, when players such as Alfredo Di Stéfano, Ferenc Puskás and Francisco Gento helped Real to win the first five European Cups.

Club
Real Madrid C.F.

Typeface
Custom

Year
2011

Design
Sporting iD

Designer
Anthony Barnett

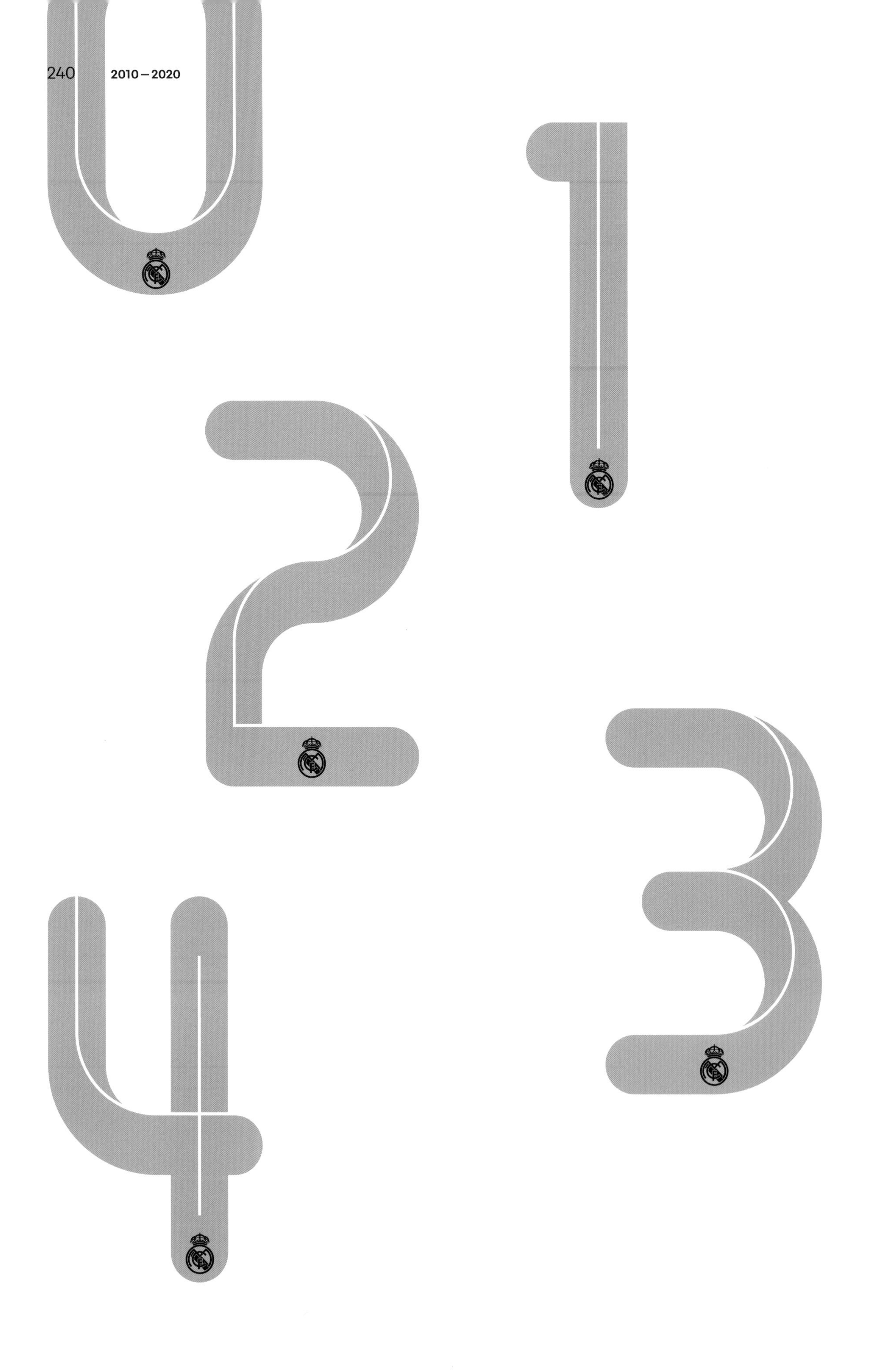

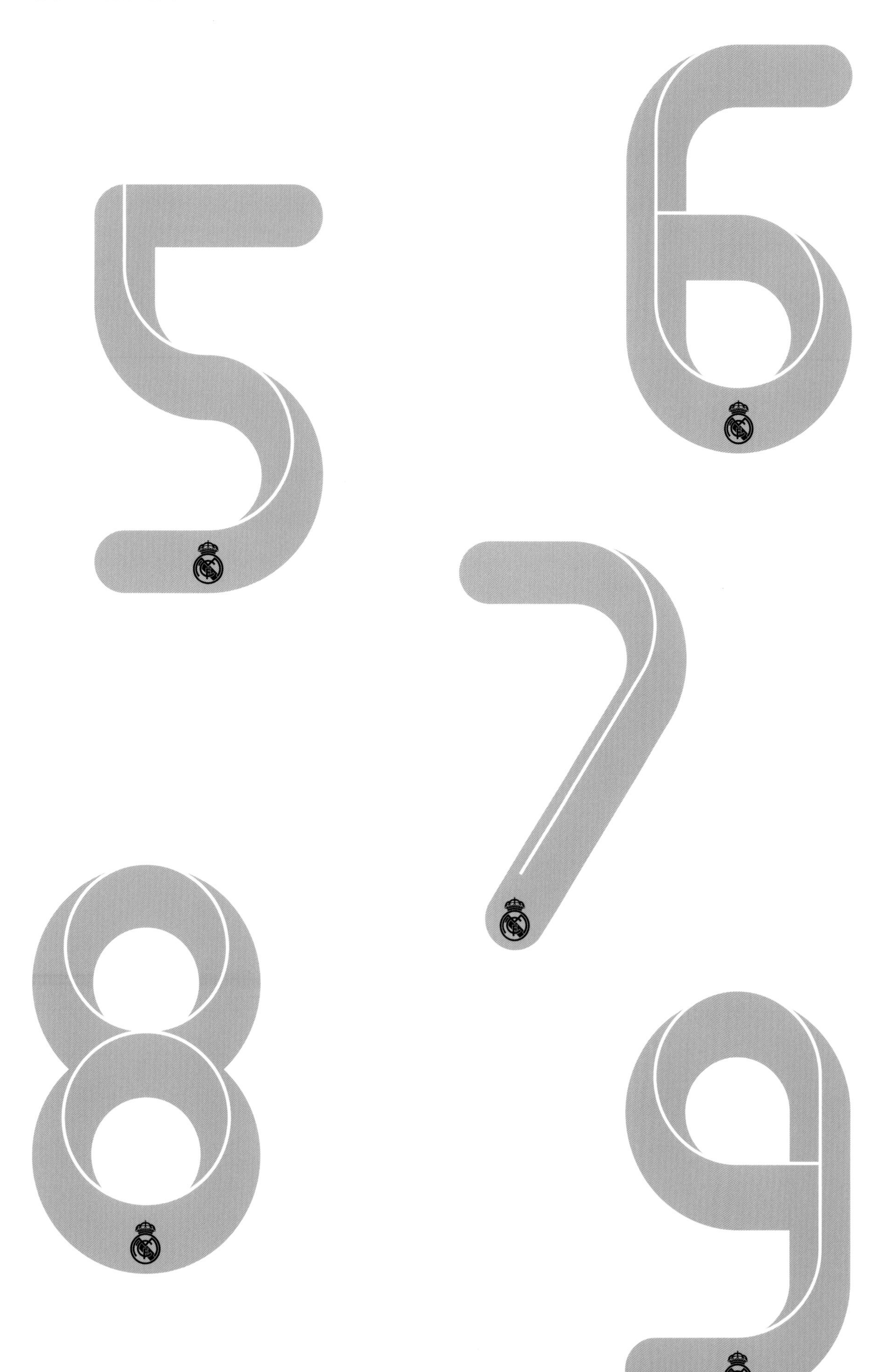

KANOUTE
12
LFP
SFC

While a number of clubs have retired the number 12 shirt in honour of its supporters ("the 12th man"), in 2011 Sevilla came up with a different way to allow fans to be part of the action – and to raise revenue too.

In collaboration with Playing2, the club offered supporters the chance to have a 2×2mm picture of themselves form part of their chosen player's number for €24.90. "People do seem willing to pay for the chance to be on the back of their idol," said a club spokesperson.

With an estimated 3,142 images per figure, there was approximately €75,000 at stake for each digit – did the club discourage players from wearing 1-9, we wonder? Fellow Spanish side Granada and the Wales national rugby union team later adopted the practice.

Club
Sevilla FC

Typeface
Custom

Year
2011

ROBINHO

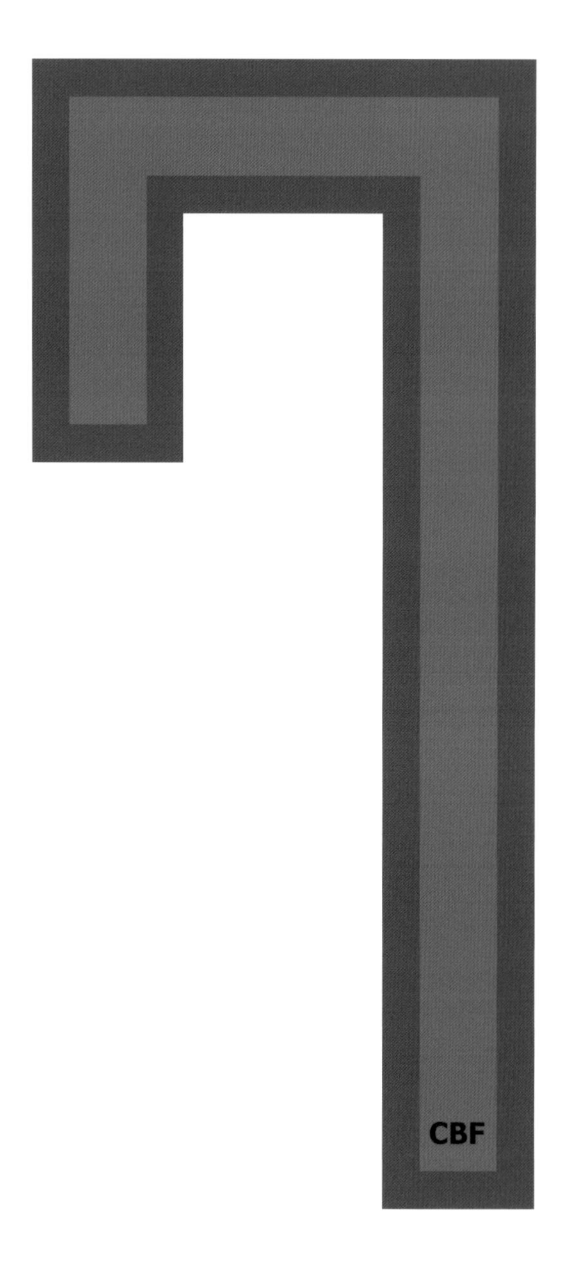

Country
Brazil

Typeface
Custom

Year
2011

Design
Nike

RAMIRES

Estonia performed well in the Euro 2012 qualifiers, finishing second to Italy in their group, ahead of Serbia, Slovenia, Northern Ireland and the Faroe Islands.

Could the good showing have had anything to do with the bespoke numbering and lettering introduced? Mart Anderson came up with the new design, which drew on the distinct Estonian national character.

Based on the Estonian tradition of stone-carving, the angular shapes look simple but are in fact based on a strict system of rake angles — each adjacent letter fits together in a mosaic-like fashion to form a complete pattern. While the new typography was instantly recognisable to Estonians, it was new and fresh on the world stage.

Captain Ragnar Klavan was certainly impressed: "Creating a special typeface for the shirts of the Estonian national team is a way of showing support to the team," he said. "It is very important from the players' point of view: it brings this warm and fuzzy feeling, gives you strength, makes you think about Estonia and all the people who support us and whom we represent. In the international arena it is important to demonstrate our culture, for football is not just a sports show, football is a universal language."

Unfortunately for Estonia, they would miss out on a place in the finals in Poland and Ukraine as they lost to the Republic of Ireland in a play-off.

Photography
Jana Pipar

RESPECT
LUTS
13

Country
Estonia

Typeface
Hanse

Year
2012

Designer
Mart Anderson

ABCDEFGHIJKL
MNOPQRSTUVWXYZ
abcdefghijklmno
pqrstuvwxyz
0123456789
!@()*€?:;

AN1ER

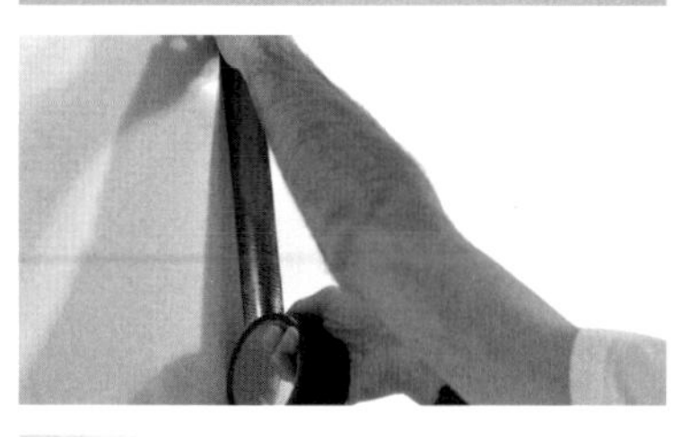

Let's face it, in an amateur dressing room, you're never too far away from hearing the question, "Anyone got any tape?"

If PUMA's 2012 font looked like it was created from gaffer tape, that's because it was. London design studio GBH's campaign concept was 'Make Football Anywhere' and it delved into the heart of the sport, and the use of tape to secure nets and shinpads among other things, to create a novel typeface.

"GBH were clear from the start that the spirit of raw, passionate enthusiasm expressed in the campaign needed to be communicated through the typeface," GBH's Jason Gregory said.

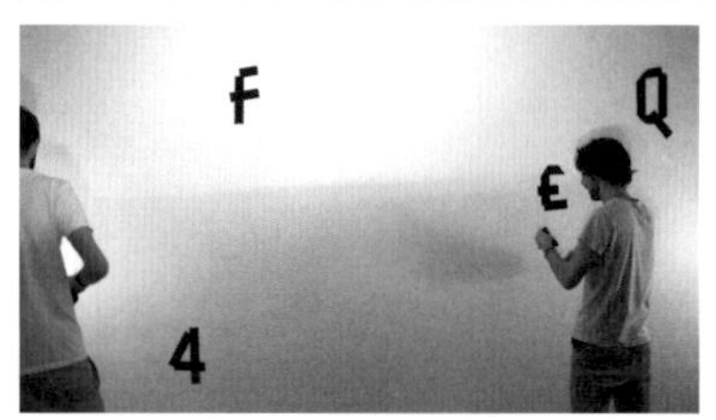

"We designed a font made of gaffer tape. We ordered 150 rolls of tape and began folding, ripping and sticking it into shapes. We created a full Roman alphabet and numerals. Dalton Maag came on board to develop the full character set and add European accents.

"The finished result was unique and stood out on the pitch due to its legibility and brevity."

Countries
Names & numbers for all PUMA teams

Typeface
Gaffer

Year
2012

Design
GBH

Designers
Mark Bonner & Jacob Vanderkar

Font Developer
Dalton Maag

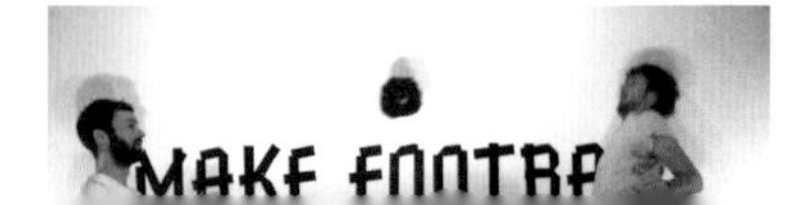

'GAFFER'

ABCDEFGHIJKLM
NOPQRSTUVWXYZ
abcdefghijklm
nopqrstuvwxyz
0123456789

ÀÁÂÃÄÅÆÇÈÉÊËÌÍÎÏÐÑÒÓÔÕÖ×ØÙÚÛÜÝÞßàáâãäåæ
çèéêëìíîïðñòóôõöùúûüýþÿĀĂĄāăąĆĈĊČćĉċčĎĐďđ
ĒĔĖĘĚēĕėęěĜĞĠĢĝğġģĤĥħĦĨĪĬĮİĩīĭįĲĳĴĵĶķĸĹĻĽĿŁ
ĺļľŀłŃŅŇŉŊńņňŋŌŎŐōŏőŒœŔŖŘŕŗřŚŜŞŠȘśŝşș š
ŢŤȚŦţțťŧŨŪŬŮŰŲũūŭůűŴẂẄẃẅŵỲŶŸŷỳŹŻŽźżž

?¿!"#$%&'()*+÷-.,/:;<=>[\]^`{}~—
¡¢£¤¥§¨©ª«¬®¯°±_´µ¶·¸
»'',"",„†‡•…‰‹›/€™Ω∂∆∏∑–/·√∞∫≈≠≤≥◊¼½¾

drogba

pienaar

asamoah

song

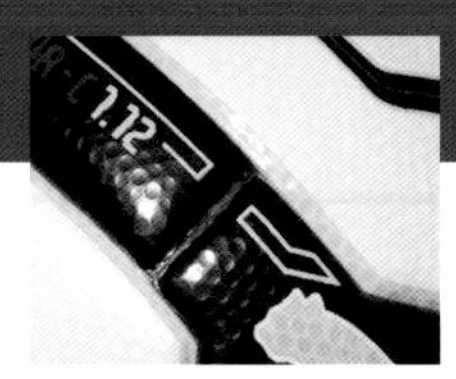
1.12

PWR-C 1.12

zokora
5
11
19

GAFFER
POWER

10

GAFFER
SPEED

10

GAFFER
ITALIA

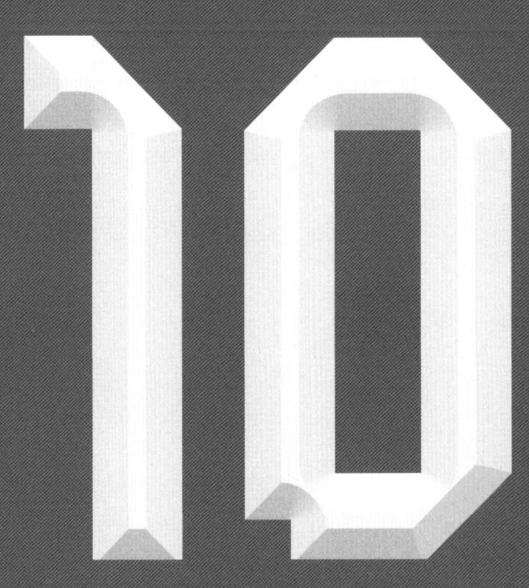

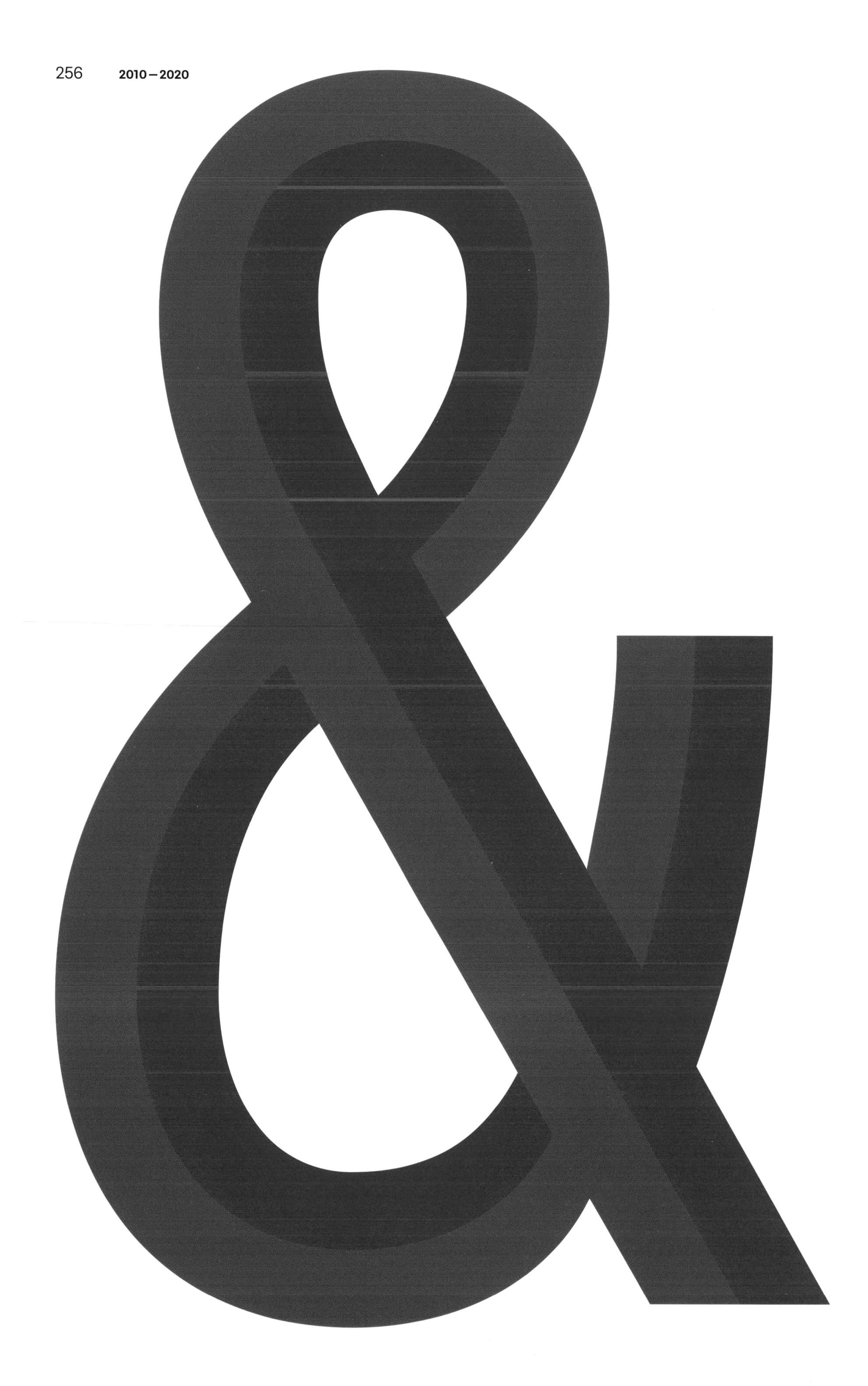

England's kit for Euro 2012 featured no blue at all, with the famous Three Lions crest rendered in white and red, and the typography was in a pleasing two-tone style, matching the collar trim and the design campaign.

Created by Paul Barnes of Commercial Type and Robert Warner, who led Umbro's design team, the numbers and letters had their roots in the 19th century, when football's rules were codified and the first international games were played.

Barnes visited St Bride Library on London's Fleet St so as to examine wood-letter examples from posters and billboards. An 1869 creation from Manchester wood-letter manufacturer Benjamin Brierly stood out, while the 1966 World Cup-winning style [p31] was used as an inspiration too. The finished article evoked the hand-made sign lettering so common among English shops and pubs and at the same time gave an impression of dimensionality.

The typeface was christened 'Vaughton' in honour of Howard Vaughton (1861-1937), the first player to score five goals in a game for England, doing so against Ireland in 1882. The feat has only been matched on three other occasions and never bettered.

Country
England

Typeface
Vaughton

Year
2012

Design
Commercial Type

Type Designer
Paul Barnes

Creative Director, Umbro
Rob Warner

Design Director, Umbro
Stewart Curran

ABCDEF
GHIJKLMN
OPQRSTUV
WXYZ
1234567890
&,.“”‘’;:!?

BENT
9

A. INIESTA

As had become the practice, for Euro 2012 adidas employed the same font across its roster, including Spain — who retained their title for a third straight major-finals victory, having also won the 2010 World Cup — Germany, joint-hosts Ukraine, Denmark, Greece and Russia.

Designed by Christian Binger, a very subtle shadow effect was created with a series of narrow diagonal lines to give the impression of a lighter section from a distance. The typeface also featured on the official match ball for the tournament, the Tango 12. While the new ball's construction was modern, based on the Jabulani from the 2010 World Cup, the look was decidedly retro, with the three-point shapes referencing the classic Tango design.

1234567890

ABCDEFGHIJKLMNOPQRSTUVWXYZß !"#'*,- /^'~°()=+:><?%,,^ŠŒŽ¯i

ÀÁÂÃÄÅÆÇŞ

ÈÉÊĚËÌÍÎÏĐÑŅĻĢĀ

ÒÓÔǑÕÖØ

ÙÚÛǓÜÝŸ

Countries
Names & numbers for all adidas teams

Typeface
adidas Euro 2012

Year
2012

Design
adidas

Design Director, adidas
Christian Binger

Under Pep Guardiola, Barcelona were the team of the turn of the decade from the 2000s to 2010s, with Champions League victories in 2009 and 2011 underlining that status, while their players backboned the Spanish sides which won Euro 2008, the 2010 World Cup and Euro 2012.

When Nike commissioned Studio Vasava to create a new Barça typeface in 2012, the brief was to reflect the club's style for quick, high-energy football – while Guardiola had departed, his creation lived on.

Vasava were inspired by legendary architect Antoni Gaudí, whose work can be seen throughout the city. Gaudí's subtle cuts and chimney angles fed into the new typeface, connecting Barcelona's cultural history with the club.

Club
FC Barcelona

Typeface
FCB 2013

Year
2012

Design
Vasava

Designer
Bruno Selles

01234
56789
ABCDEFGHIJKLMN
OPQRSTUVWXYZÇ

Hungarian motion and graphic designer David Sum created Borg and, unusually, made it available for free download.

He describes it as "a geometric typeface with a curved incision. My inspiration was Swedish furniture."

Greek side PAOK used this font for the 2015-16 season and it certainly proved popular as it was adopted by Levante of Spain, Italian side Napoli and France's Paris Saint-Germain the following year.

Clubs
PAOK FC (2015)
Levante UD (2016)
S.S.C. Napoli (2016)
Paris Saint-Germain F.C. (2016)

Typeface
Borg

Year
2013

Design
David Sum

MAX 11

J. MORALES 8

JORGINHO 8

VERRATTI 6

While FIFA mandate that each player wearing Nº 1 at a World Cup must be a goalkeeper, there is no such rule in the English football league.

In 1993-94, when the Premier League introduced squad numbers, the Football League made them optional and Charlton Athletic, one of the clubs to go with the system, decided to list their players alphabetically, meaning defender Stuart Balmer wore 1 with goalkeeper Bob Bolder assigned the Nº 2 shirt.

When Brian Clough was manager of Nottingham Forest, he began to wear an emerald green jumper on the sideline. The origins of this were as a result of him ensuring that his authority wasn't usurped.

Having signed Peter Shilton for a record fee, he felt that the goalkeeper (and everyone else) needed reminding of who the boss was. At training one day, he donned a top in the colour traditionally worn by the keepers and said to Shilton: "There's only one number 1 round here, and it's not you."

As player-manager of Barnet in 2013, Edgar Davids wanted to make a similar statement, and felt that that was best achieved by actually wearing Nº 1 on the field. In addition, he demanded a font similar to that used by the Netherlands at Euro 2000 — we can't guarantee that copyright laws weren't broken.

The previous inhabitant of 1, Liam O'Brien, had left the club and so nobody was displaced by this decision. Unfortunately for Davids, it didn't really have any inspirational effect as he was sent off three times before the end of December and resigned on January 18, 2014.

Country
Netherlands

Typefaces
Din (Names) &
Custom (Numbers)

Year
2000

Design
Nike

Photography
footballshirtcollective.com

Club
Barnet F.C.

Typefaces
Din (Names) &
Custom (Numbers)

Year
2013

DAVIDS

PSG-LIGHT
ABCDEFGHIJKLMNOPQRSTUVWXYZ
abcdefghijklmnopqrstuvwxyz
0123456789
-/:;()$&@.,?!‘’”[]{}#%^*+=_\—<>€£¥

PSG-REGULAR
ABCDEFGHIJKLMNOPQRSTUVWXYZ
abcdefghijklmnopqrstuvwxyz
0123456789
-/:;()$&@.,?!‘’”[]{}#%^*+=_\—<>€£¥

PSG-BOLD
ABCDEFGHIJKLMNOPQRSTUVWXYZ
abcdefghijklmnopqrstuvwxyz
0123456789
-/:;()$&@.,?!‘’”[]{}#%^*+=_\—<>€£¥

PSG-INLINE
ABCDEFGHIJKLMNOPQRSTUVWXYZ
0123456789
-/:;()$&.,?!‘’”[]{}#%^*+=\<>€

Given a brief to come up with a complete overhaul of Paris Saint-Germain's imagery, including its crest, design agency Dragon Rouge commissioned Paris/Casablanca font foundry Babelfont to create a typeface.

Inspired by typographies from the 1940s, the font, 'PSG' is intended to embody a strong club image, one deeply rooted in its origins. A modern flourish is added with the versatility of the font, which could be altered to light, bold and inline versions.

In 2018, PSG entered into a partnership with Air Jordan, an off-shoot of Nike. A special line of Champions League kits and merchandise was produced, with Jordan's 'Jumpman' logo featuring prominently.

Club
Paris Saint-Germain F.C.

Typeface
PSG

Year
2014

Design
Dragon Rouge

Type Design
Babelfont

Club
Real Madrid C.F.

Typeface
RM14/15

Year
2014

Design
Sporting iD

Designer
Jonathan Dykes

8

While recent years haven't been as kind to AC Milan on the field as the glory days of the late 1980s through the 1990s and into the 2000s, off the field there is a continued creativity at play.

For 2014-15, each of the club's three shirts featured a different crest, showing bravery to promote separate identities rather than feeling the need to bring everything under the banner of a single brand.

On the backs of those shirts was the corporate Milan Type font, which was used in a variety of instances, such as the signage at the club's Milanello training ground, logo lockups, restaurants and various digital applications. This was designed by Antonio Pace, who in 2002 designed a logotype and font for the city of Milan.

Club
A.C. Milan

Typeface
Milan Type

Year
2014

Design
Inarea

Type Design
Antonio Pace

Milan Type Regular

AΛBCDEFGHIJKLMNOPQRSTUVWXYZ
abcdefghijklmnopqrstuvwxyz
0123456789
--?:;()$€£¥&&@.,?!',"[]{}#%^*+=_\|<>

Milan Type Bold

AΛBCDEFGHIJKLMNOPQRSTUVWXYZ
abcdefghijklmnopqrstuvwxyz
0123456789
--?:;()$€£¥&&@.,?!',"[]{}#%^*+=_\|<>

1 - GABRIEL

2 - DE SCIGLIO

4 - R. ELY

5 - BONAVENTURA

7 - L. ADRIANO

8 - SUSO

9 - LAPADULA

10 - HONDA

11- NIANG

13 - ROMAGNOLI

14 - MATI

15 - GÓMEZ

16 - POLI

17 - ZAPATA

18 - MONTOLIVO

20 - ABATE

21 - VAGIONI

23 - SOSA

29 - PALETTA

31 - ANTONELLI

33 - KUCO

35 - PLIZZARI

70 - BACCA

73 - LOCATELLI

90 - PAŠALIĆ

91 - BERTOLACCI

96 - CALABRIA

99 - DONNARUMMA

Photography
Studio Buzzi

GABRIEL
1
R. ELY
4
NIANG
11
GOMEZ
15

Club
Inter Milan

Typeface
Inter Metric

Year
2014

Design
Leftloft

Type Design
Kris Sowersby
& Dave Foster

TER

Not to be outdone, AC Milan's rivals Inter also sought a clearly identifiable and consistent typeface for all of its activities.

The 'Inter Metric' font was created by Leftloft alongside type designer Kris Sowersby. "In bringing this new identity to life, we wanted to create a highly contemporary image for a historical team, by celebrating both football values and traditions," they said.

"In order to talk about 106 years of history, we first had to deal with bringing together many different products and identities. To develop a coherent strategy, we focused on five strong values that define Inter's personality: Milanese, international, legendary, surprising, loyal.

"The entire rebranding process was conceived with the purpose of creating a versatile but unique identity; combining a strong modern personality, with a careful review of iconic and traditional elements."

abcdefghij
klmnopqrst
uvwxyzßfffifl
ABCDEFGH
IJKLMNOPQ
RSTUVWXYZ
$€£0123456789
?1&§©℗™®

INTER
Channel

INTER
Forever

INTER
Academy

INTER
Centro di
Formazione

INTER
Club

INTER
Scuola
Calcio

INTER
Summer
Camp

INTER
Campus

JAVI FUEGO
18

Club
Valencia CF

Typeface
VCF Types

Year
2014

Type Design
Valencia CF (Graphic Design Department)

Photography
Lázaro de la Peña (official VCF Photographer)

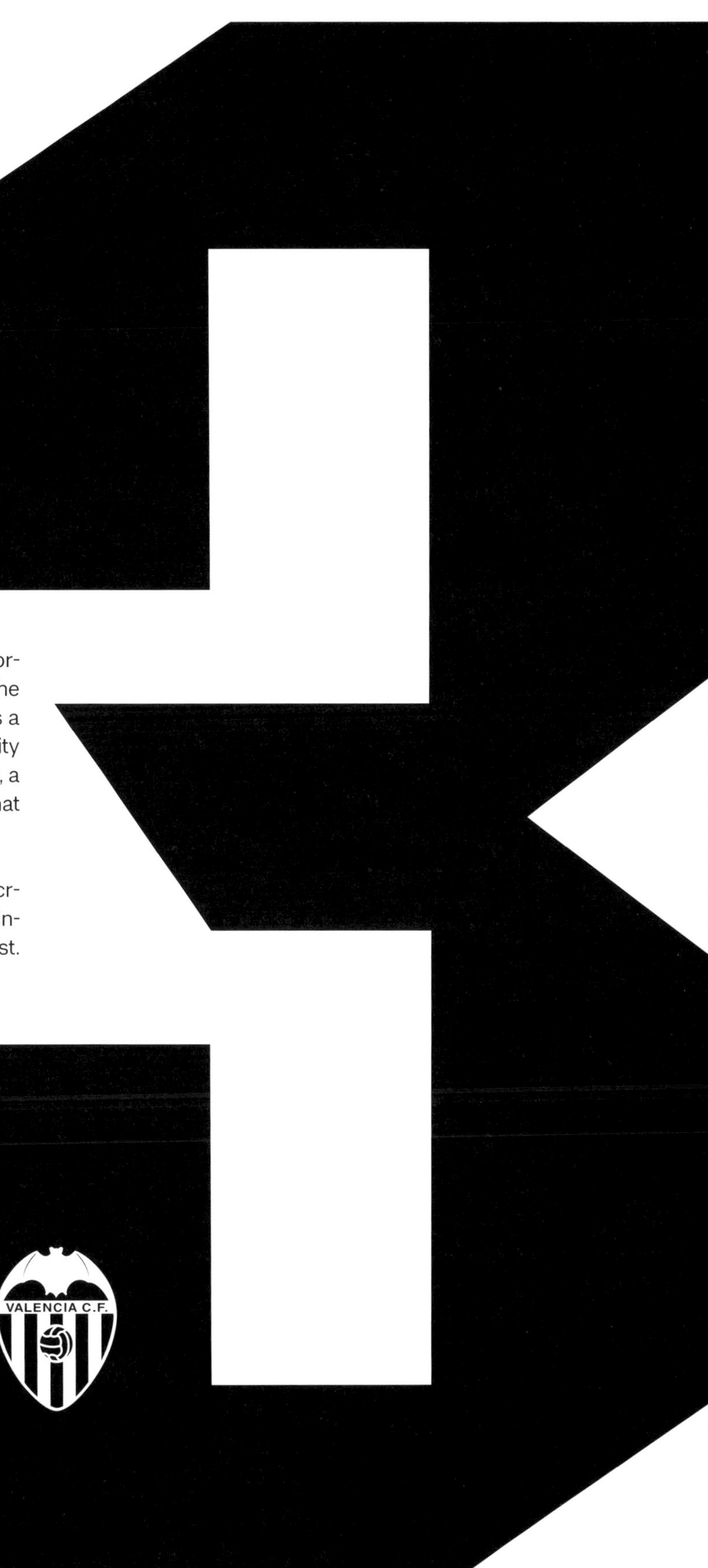

Symbolism and history are important to Valencia CF, whose crest features the bat from the city's coat of arms. There is a theory that, as King James I entered the city in 1238, re-conquering it from the Moors, a bat landed on his flag and he interpreted that as a good sign.

For 2014-15, Los Murciélagos ('The Bats') created a new angular and aggressive font in-house, featuring a monochrome club crest.

012
3456
789

A B C D E F G
H I J K L M N Ñ
O P Q R S T U V
W X Y Z Ç . ` ´ -

Photography
Lazaro de la Peña

For the 2014 World Cup in Brazil, adidas's name and number style was influenced by the wishbands of Bahia, a design feature also prominent on the Brazuca matchball and on the backs and sides of the countries' shirts.

Hand-made trial versions were used at the beginning of the design process.

Countries
Names & numbers
for all adidas teams

Typeface
adidas WC 2014

Year
2014

Design
adidas

Senior Designer, adidas
Martin Tibabuzo

Senior Design Director, adidas
Jürgen Rank

ABCDEFGHIJKLMNOPQRSTUVWXYZ

Floor Wesseling was the designer at the centre of Brazil's kits and typography for the 2014 World Cup, which the country hosted.

"This was the most difficult one to do during that season," he says, "making something unfamiliar to my own handwriting or style but suitable and identifying to the Brazilian population.

"Together with Stuart McArthur, my creative director at the time who did a lot of research on Brazil culture, we looked at many classic, popular and modern Brazilian typefaces and Brazilian architecture, like the work of Niemeyer or Weinfeld (typical Brazilian names, right?!).

"'fundição Brasil' means something like the melting pot or more literal welder of Brazil. It suited the idea of unity and it made us think of an old iron or wooden typeset used for 'high print'. The shape of the numbers sometimes make me itch but they work really well and they were very much appreciated by the CBF."

ABCÇDEFG
HIJKLMN
OPQRSTÚ
VWXYZ

123
456
7890

Country
Brasil

Typeface
fundição Brasil

Year
2014

Design
Nike

Lead Designer, Nike
Floor Wesseling

Creative Director, Nike
Stuart McArthur

NEYMAR

Renowned designer Neville Brody collaborated with Nike to create England's font for the 2014 World Cup, which was named 'Case Brody'.

"It has been an extraordinary honour to design the fonts for the England national team," he said.

"The core inspiration was to focus on the intersection between flair and workmanlike reliability. Small touches emphasize the idea of innovation, invention and surprise, built around a more geometric structure.

"The industrialized suggestion of a stencil was simultaneously based on a pinstripe motif, combining style with no-frills efficiency."

Country
England

Typeface
Case Brody

Year
2014

Designer
Neville Brody

Country
Netherlands

Typeface
Case Crouwel

Year
2014

Design
Nike

Designers, Nike
Floor Wesseling
with Wim Crouwel

123
456
7890

BLIND
5

A design legend was also involved with the Dutch numbering, as the late Wim Crouwel created Case Crouwel, assisted by Floor Wesseling.

"It was a great design process, where I was able to work with one of my design heroes and one of the most famous designers of Holland. The man is an institution," Wesseling says.

"The classic Dutch typographic stamps from the early 1980s were the inspiration initially and the starting point for the work. During the process we worked digitally, where Wim guided with pencil on the prints. It was a real pleasure."

SNEIJDER

Floor Wesseling also had the 2014 Portuguese font to his credit.

"It was a great honour to work for the FPF, the Portuguese federation," he says, "especially as it means working for maybe the best player in the world, Cristiano Ronaldo.

"It was my first season working for the FPF, not knowing yet that 'CR7' had a big say in the result. We were making embroidered crests on the players' shirts but Ronaldo preferred a sticker, or 'stampa' to avoid any irritation.

"That then became the motivation for the typeface and quite quickly I had the feeling of which way to go, combining smooth curves with straight sticks. At first, I had sharp gaps taken out of the letters referring to Ronaldo's haircut at the time, but he did not appreciate that, so the Stampa became a solid rocker, smooth enough to be Portuguese, approved by Cristiano himself."

123
456
7890

ÃBCDEFG
HIJKLMNOP
QRSTUV
WXYZ

Country
Portugal

Typeface
Ronaldo Stampa

Year
2014

Design
Nike

Designer, Nike
Floor Wesseling

RONALDO

DROGBA

PUMA had already been using a square sans serif called 'Geogrotesque' in its communications and the company wanted something similar on shirts for the 2014 World Cup. London design studio GBH commissioned Eduardo Manso to create such a typeface.

"Basically, the concept was to incorporate the marks of the football pitch into a condensed version of Geogrotesque, without being too literal," he said. "We replaced all diagonals by subtle curves, so it still refers to the pitch, but preserves the legibility while creating a unique personality too. It was also crucial to properly differentiate similar-looking numbers like 6, 8 and 9 for example, to avoid confusing the football commentators or the people announcing the substitutions. It has a nice but unusually long name — Nature of Believing — that matches PUMA's World Cup campaign."

Countries
Names & numbers for all PUMA teams

Typeface
Geogrotesque (Nature of Believing)

Year
2014

Design
GBH

Type Designer
Eduardo Manso

Designer, PUMA
Ulrich Planer

NATURE OF BELIEVING

ABCDEFGHIJKLM
NOPQRSTUVWXYZ
0123456789

AÁÀÄBCÇDEÉÈËFG
HIÍÌÏJKLMNOÓÒÖ
PQRSTUÚÙÜVWXYZ
L'A L-A P.D

12
345
67890

In 1939, after the Spanish Civil War, Levante FC had a lot of players but nowhere to play while Gimnástico FC were short on human resources but possessed the historic Estadio de Vallego.

A merger to form Levante UD was the best solution for all and led to the creation of the nickname Los Granotas ('the frogs') as the stadium was located next to an old riverbed. It was generally dry but when puddles appeared, so did the frogs. The name stuck and green has often been used as a colour for change kits.

In 2014, it therefore made perfect sense for Jorge Lawerta to incorporate a frog-skin pattern into the club's numbers.

Club
Levante UD

Typeface
Levante 14

Year
2014

Designer
Jorge Lawerta

After 20 years with Nike, Arsenal entered into a partnership with PUMA in 2014. The new two-tone blue third kit with green accents had an unusual diagonal-striped style, and this formed the basis for the numbers on the home, away and third kits, with a customised version of the standard 'Geogrotesque' font.

Club
Arsenal F.C.

Typeface
Geogrotesque (Customised)

Year
2014

Design
PUMA

Designer, PUMA
Ulrich Planer

ABCDEFGHIJKLM
NOPQRSTUVWXYZ
0123456789

GIROUD

PUMA also customised the Geogrotesque font for Borussia Dortmund. Like many other German teams, they used the keyline-shadow after its introduction in the 1970s and into the 1980s, but PUMA tailored it to the 'Die Borussen' by having rounded edges, tying in with the club's circular crest.

A special Eszett or 'double-s' character (ß) had to be created for Kevin Großkreutz.

Club
Borussia Dortmund

Typeface
Geogrotesque (Customised)

Year
2015

Design
PUMA

Designer, PUMA
Ulrich Planer

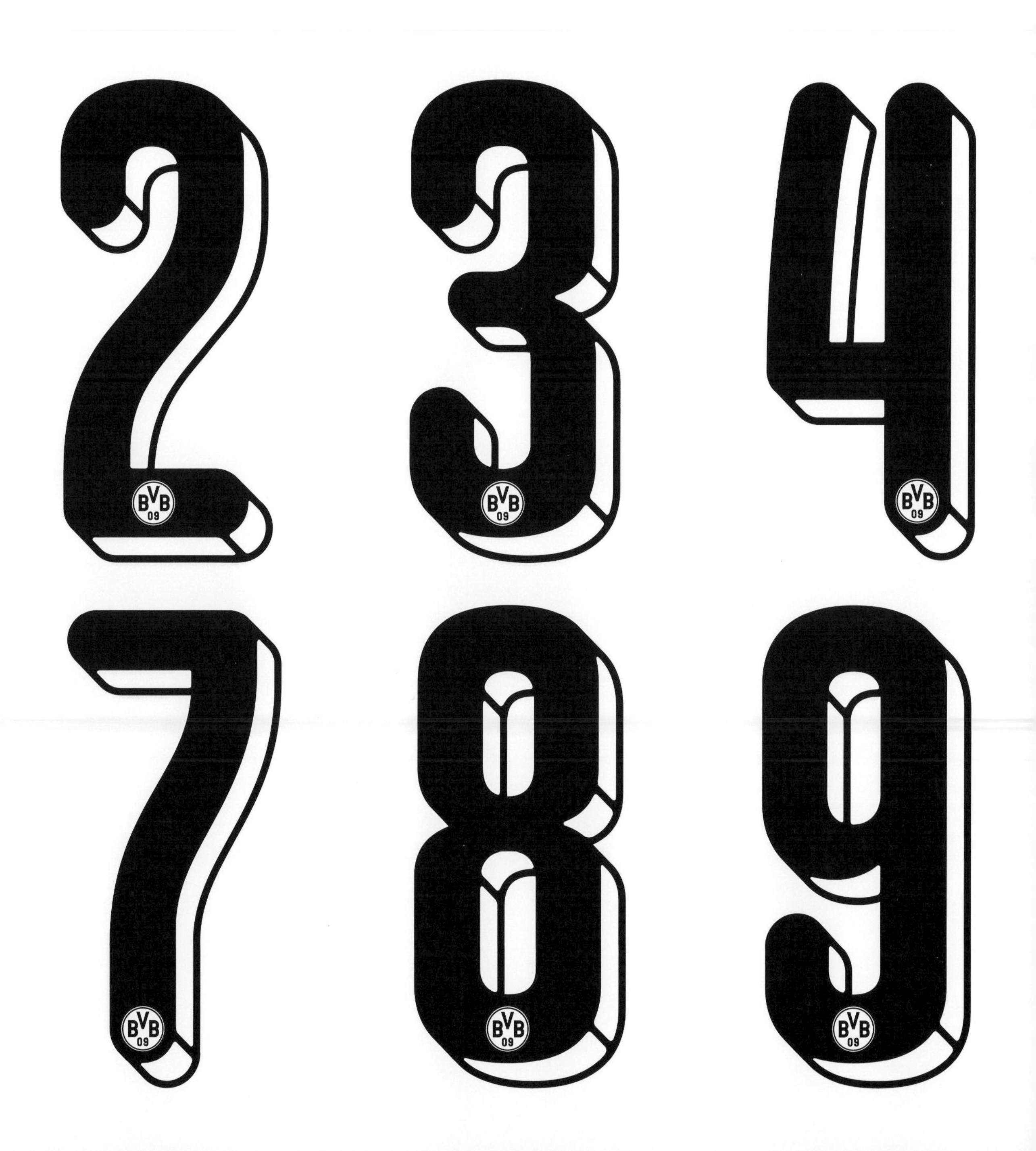
2
3
4
7
8
9
BVB 09
BVB 09
BVB 09
BVB 09
BVB 09
BVB 09

When Wolfsburg took on Borussia Dortmund in the DFB-Pokal final on May 30, 2015, three interested viewers were Christoph Koeberlin, Hannes von Döhren and Livius Dietzel. Not because any of the three were fans of either club, though.

Shortly beforehand, Volkswagen's new corporate typeface, designed by von Döhren and Dietzel and produced by Koeberlin, had been launched and they were keen to see it on the advertising boards.

Wolfsburg won the cup for the first time and, just as much a celebration for the trio, was what they noticed during the game — the players' names and numbers on the backs of the shirts was also in the VW typeface!

However, such guerrilla marketing was against German league rules and so the practice didn't continue in the 2015-16 season.

Club
VfL Wolfsburg

Typeface
VW Type

Year
2015

Type Designer
Hannes von Döhren

The crest of PSV (Philips Sport Vereniging) has a flag as its central feature and for 2015-16, Newminds design studio created this font, with the principle of wanting every player to proudly wear the flag.

The flag is reflected in all numbers and letters, with the notch in all characters giving the design a dynamic, fast and modern look.

Club
PSV Eindhoven

Typeface
PSV Flag bearer

Year
2015

Design
Newminds

Designer
Rinse Elsenga

PSV
EST 1913

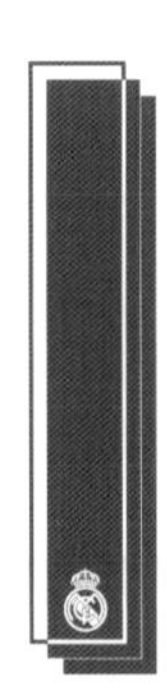

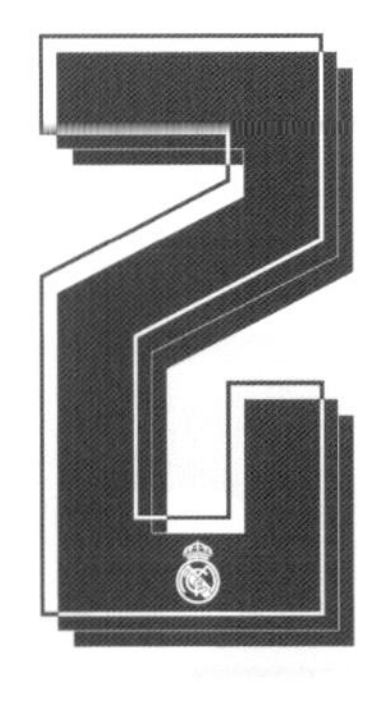

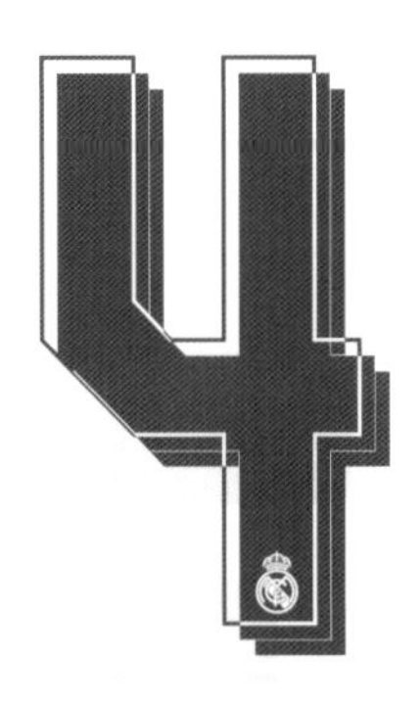

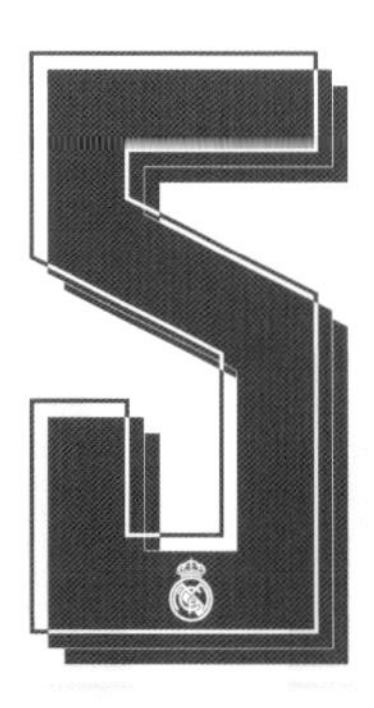

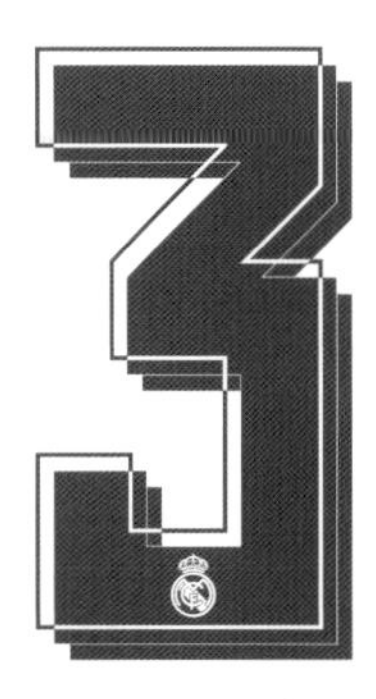

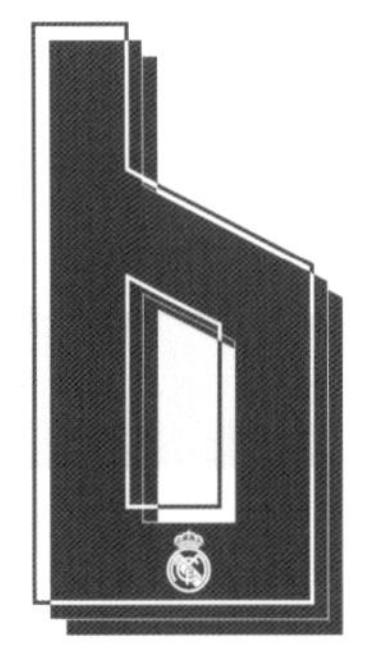

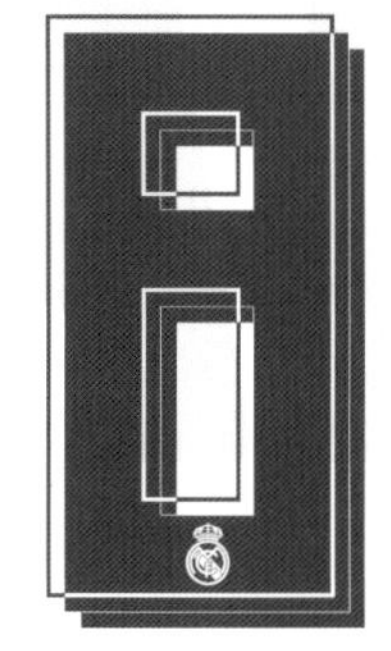

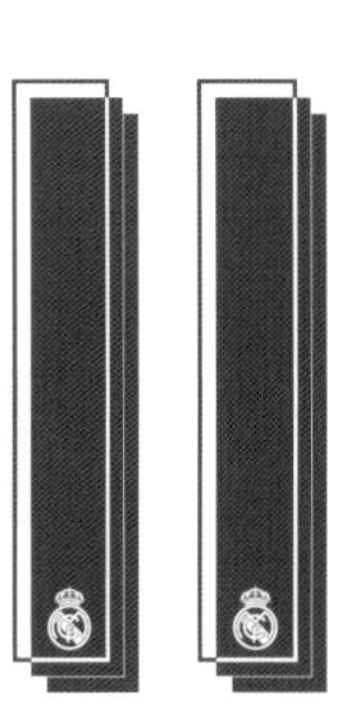

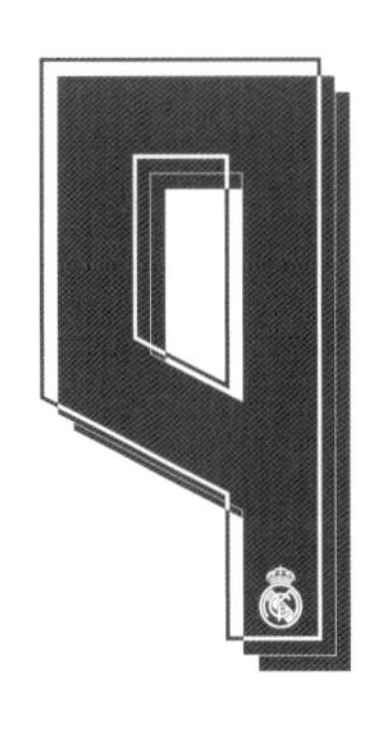

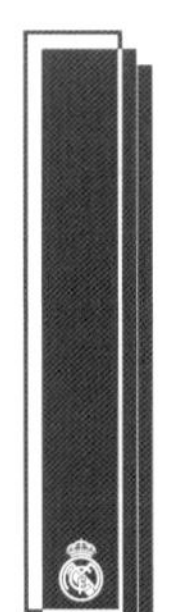

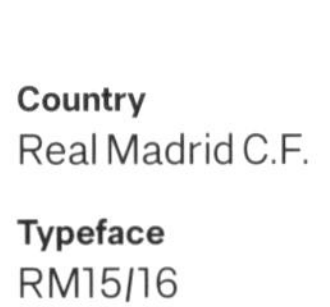

Country
Real Madrid C.F.

Typeface
RM15/16

Year
2015

Design
Sporting iD

Designer
Ian Cherry

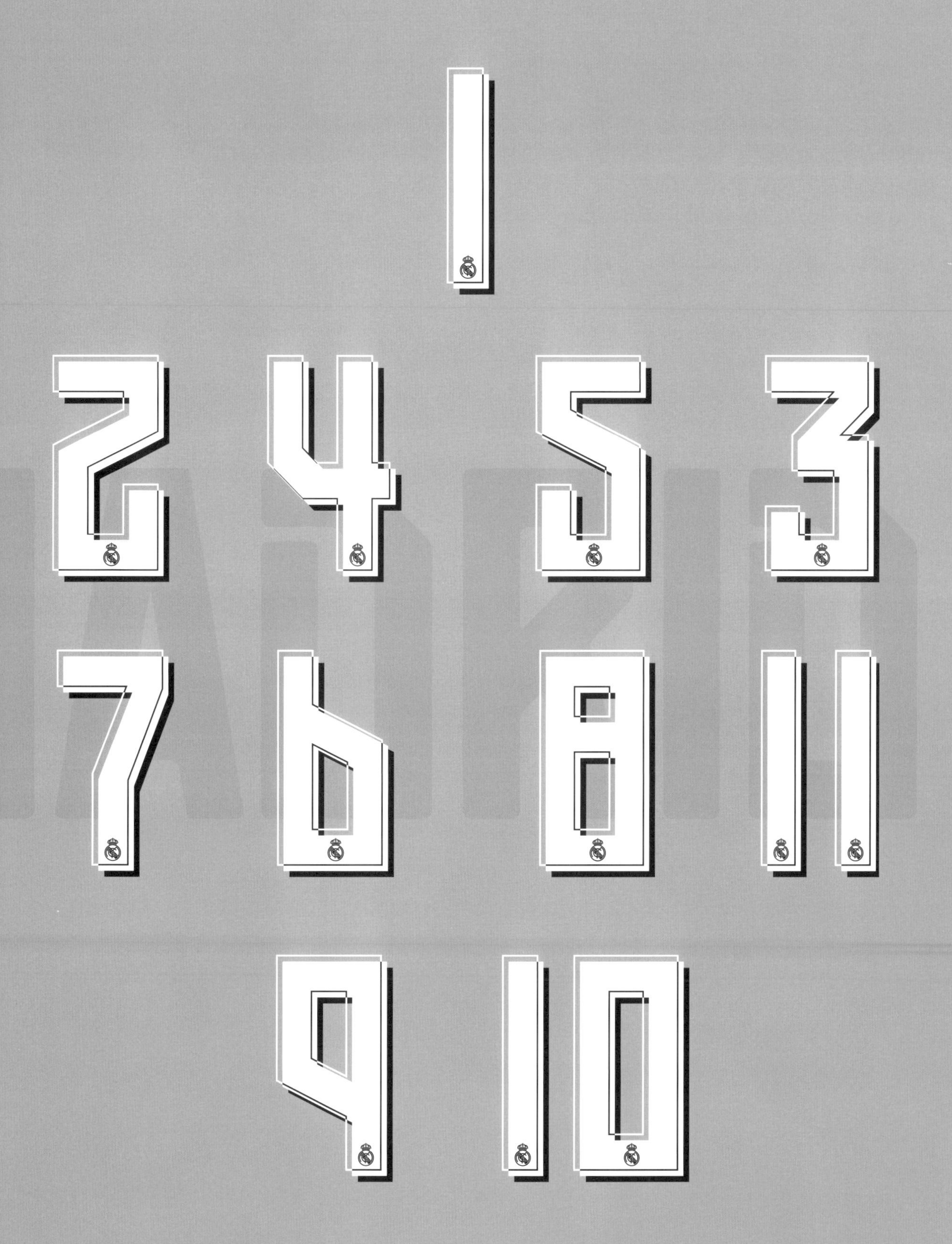
1
2 4 5 3
7 6 8 11
9 10

Canada used a uniquely tailored font for the first time at the 2015 Women's World Cup, with the design also used by the men's team in qualifiers for the 2018 World Cup.

Inspired by Canada's northern location, each character is shaped to symbolise the strength of ice that is precisely chiselled to bring its beauty to light. Appropriately named 'Les Rouges', the font was intended to embody the determination and resilience the national teams showed.

Country
Canada

Typeface
Les Rouges

Year
2015

Design
Umbro

ABCDEFGHIJKLMN
PQRSTUVWXYZ

Club
Manchester United F.C.

Typeface
MUFC 2015

Year
2015

Design
adidas

Designer, adidas
Inigo Turner

Manchester United returned to adidas after a 23-year gap in 2015, and the club's first kits back in three stripes evoked memories of those worn from 1982-84.

The numbering was similarly influenced [p86] and is reminiscent of the font seen on British vehicle number-plates. Designers Christian Jeffery and Inigo Turner had to trawl through archive video footage to make sure every number was correct.

In addition, as names on shirts weren't worn in the 1980s, a new letterset had to be created from scratch to tie in with the numbers.

012
3456
789

DE GEA

8

Arsenal

For Arsenal's second season with PUMA, 2015-16, a modified version of Geogrotesque was again used.

PUMA's inspiration came from Art Deco shapes in the interior of Emirates Stadium (in turn influenced by the old ground at Highbury) and previous club crests.

The diamond motif on the gold away shirts was the starting point for the numbers and letters, with diamonds incorporated into the glyphs.

Club
Arsenal F.C.

Typeface
Geogrotesque (customised)

Year
2015

Design
PUMA

Designer, PUMA
Ulrich Planer

ABCDEFGHIJKLM
NOPQRSTUVWXYZ

01234
56789

S. CAZORLA

Also employing Art Deco influences were Atlético Madrid in 2016.

The 2016-17 was the club's last in the Estadio Vicente Calderón before moving to the Wanda Metropolitano. Atlético were undergoing a club rebranding, with the mission to combine the past and the future and the new stadium name was an homage to previous Estadio Metropolitano de Madrid.

For the font, ticket stubs from the older Metropolitano were the influence, especially the unique 'A'. The font combined narrow angular letters with wider rounded characters.

ATM METROPOLITANA
ABCDEFGHIJKLMNOPQRSTUVWXYZ
0123456789

GRIEZMANN

Club
Atlético de Madrid

Typeface
ATM Metropolitana

Year
2016

Design
Vasava Fonts

Designers
Bruno Sellés &
Jorge Domenech

As the 2016 European Championship took place in France, Nike wanted to use the typeface 'Avant Garde' as the basis for its fonts.

However, designer Floor Wesseling really wanted to start from scratch. "Gradually, I made new letterforms after concentrating on the numbers," he says.

"As a personal touch, I made this number 4 where I cut off the little bar on the right. Once done, I continued making the entire typeface, which was going to be used on all Nike jerseys for 2016-17.

"The idea was to use the base of the number forms to fill it with a disturbing 3D lined graphic. We had some examples shown to the UEFA to check, but they were all declined due to the potential for confusion. Instead, top-tier nations received a special structured graphical inline, which was fun to create as a compromise. The numbers for the player versions were made with special breathable material and taped on the mesh back.

"Now and then, I see this set appear in the weird places, local football clubs or on the other side of the world. I quite like it apart from seeing the 3, there is still a mistake in it somehow but that's the charm of it as well!"

Countries
Names & numbers for all Nike teams

Typeface
Euro 16

Year
2016

Design
Nike

Lead Designer, Nike
Floor Wesseling

Designer, Nike
Lee Murphy

KNVB

Clubs & Countries
Names & numbers for all PUMA teams

Typeface
SS16

Year
2016

Design
PUMA

Designer, PUMA
Ulrich Planer

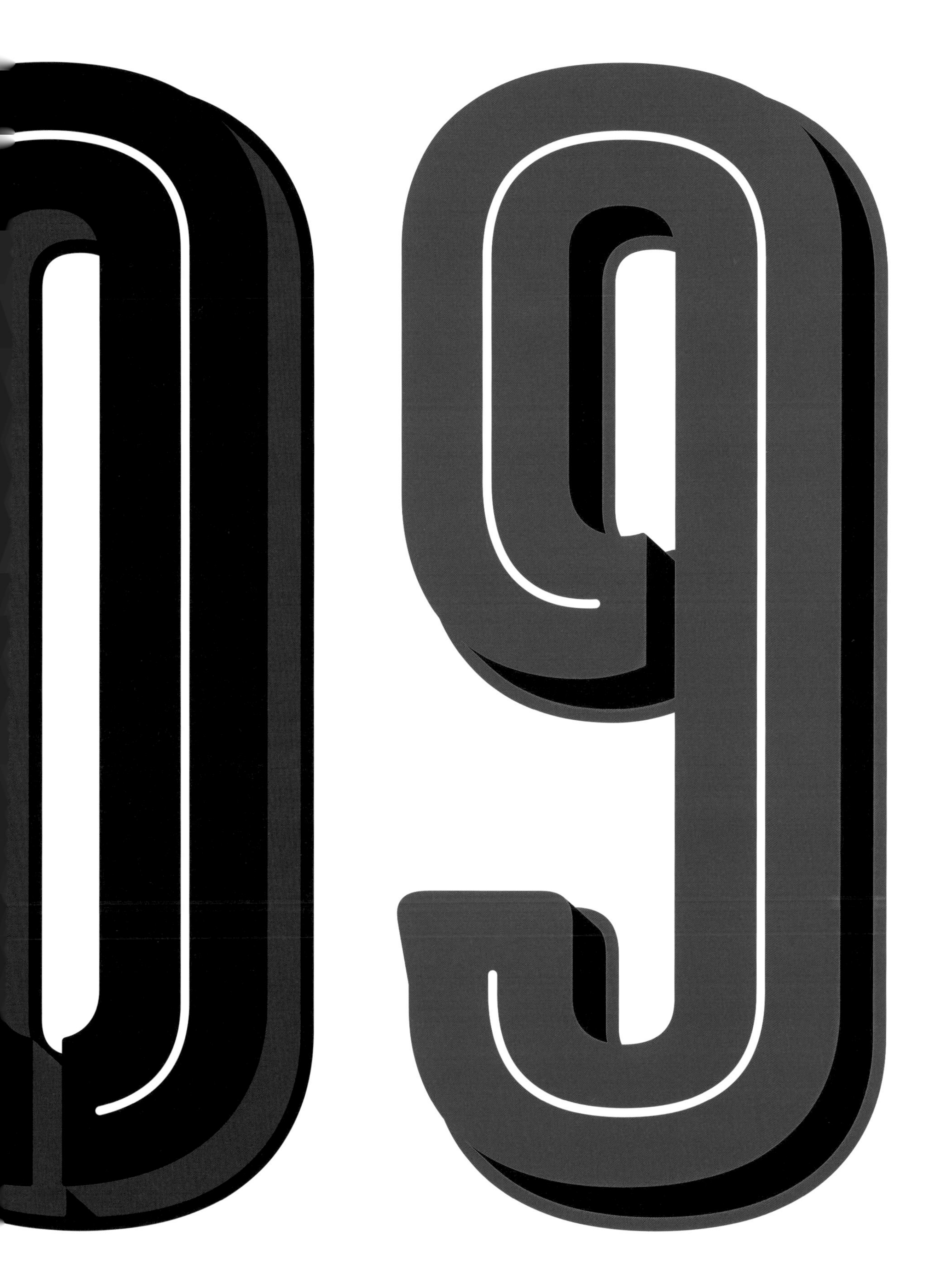

PIRLO

PUMA's slogan 'Forever Faster' was the starting point for the SS16 font, used by the company's contracts at Euro 2016.

Motorsport and race movie posters were inspirations for this typeface, with the initial intention to make it 'fast-looking' by rotating the numbers and letters by eight degrees to convey movement.

In the second stage of the design process, the team looked into shadow effects so as to make the numbers stand out more.

ABCDEFGHIJKLMNOPQRSTUVWXZY

ÀÁÂÃÄĀĂÅǺĄÆǼĆĈČĊÇDĐÈÉÊĚËĒ

ĔĖĘĜĞĠĢHĦÌÍÎĨÏĪĬİĮIJĴĶĹĽĻĿŁŃŇÑ

ŅÒÓÔÕÖŌŎŐØǾŒŔŘŖŜŠŞȘŚŤŦŢÙÚ

ÛŨÜŬŪŮŰŲẀẂŴỲÝŸŶŹŽŻŊÞß

For Euro 2016, adidas opted for a new approach in that countries had different variants of the same fonts for home and away kits. On the first-choice kits, the modern, straightforward sans-serif blended in well and didn't distract.

For the change strips, adidas allowed designers more leeway and the letterset was given a 'rawer' look, with the appearance of a spray-painted stencil, while the numbers themselves were larger.

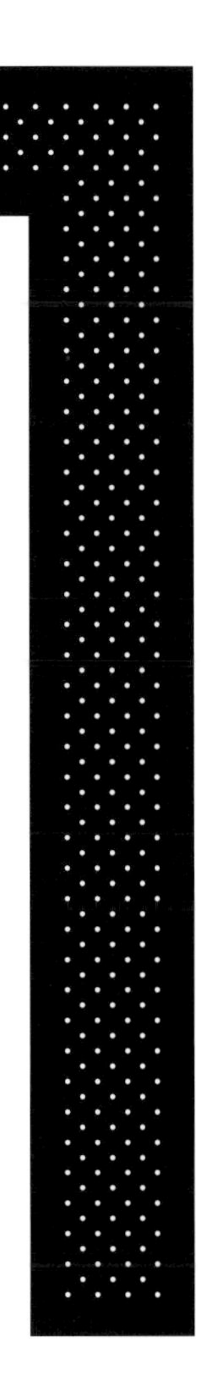

Clubs & Countries
Names & numbers for all adidas teams

Typeface
adidas Euro 2016

Year
2016

Design
adidas

Senior Designer, adidas
Martin Tibabuzo

In 2016, the English Football League (EFL) broke new ground by incorporat-
ing the logo of its official charity partner, Pro-
state Cancer UK, on its numbers.

The logo appeared for two seasons and from
the beginning of 2018-19, mental-health c-
harity Mind appeared on the newly introduced font.

In addition to the insignia on the numbers,
each player's name across all 72 EFL clubs was joined by the 'squiggle' part of the
Mind logo.

With one in four individuals affected by mental health problems, the EFL vowed to work
with its network of clubs and community t-
rusts to promote Mind's message and ser-
vices to millions nationwide, with four ambi-
tions to promote better mental health.

The partnership looks to focus on the following areas: raise awareness about mental
health with fans, clubs and staff; raise funds
to deliver life-changing support; provide support for EFL players, managers and staff;
improve the approach to mental health in the
EFL, in football and in wider society.

Brand
EFL

Typefaces
EFL 16 & 19

Year
2016 & 2019

Design
FutureBrand

Design Director
Adam Savage

Designers
George Lewis-Jones
& Vinay Mistry

Type Design
Fontsmith

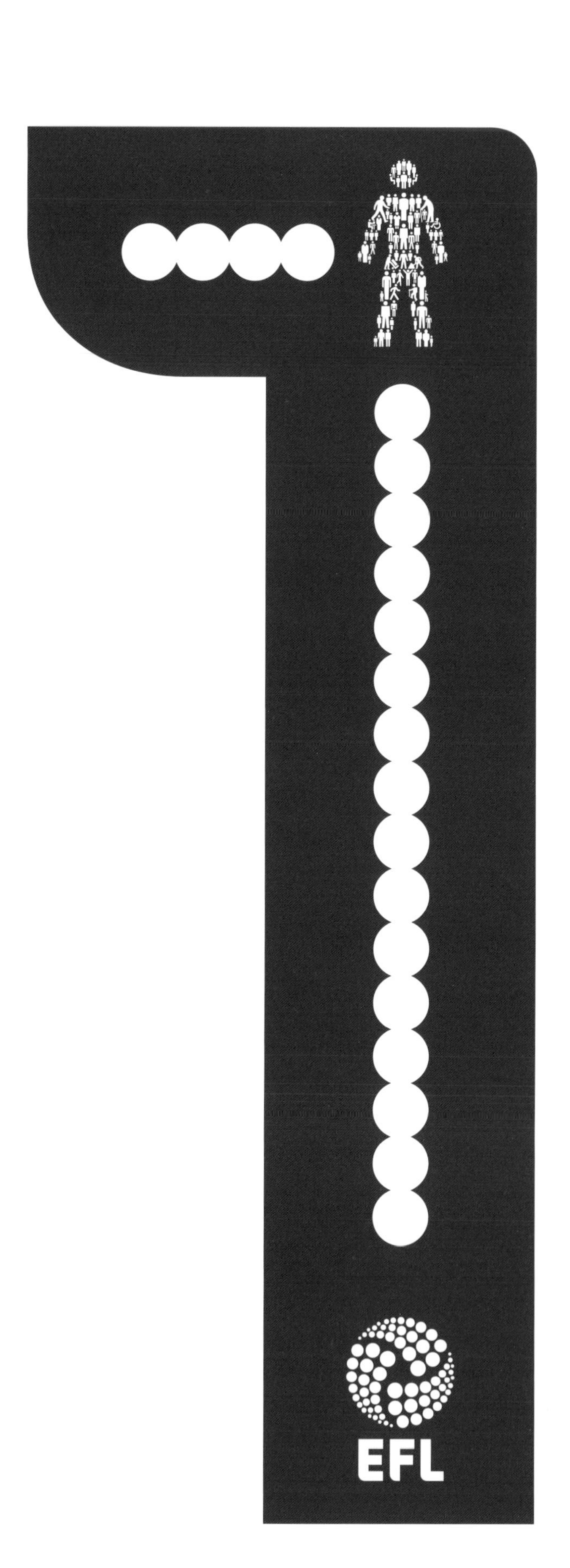

mind
EFL

Club
Exeter City F.C.

Typeface
EFL 16

Year
2017

It's the lament of many a football fan towards under-performing players: "We pay your wages."

Generally, it's not strictly true, but for a section of Exeter City fans it can be taken literally. Over the past decade, a group named the 1931 Fund — named in honour of the club's run to the FA Cup quarter-finals that season — has funded the wages of the player wearing the Nº 31 shirt.

From 2017-19, teenager Jack Sparkes had the shirt after his promotion from the youth ranks. "It is really pleasing to get the backing of the fans," he said. "The fans are what make this club and they have been really good to me and it makes me confident that when I go on the pitch I can perform well."

In the summer of 2019, Sparkes moved to Nº 22 and Noah Smerdon, who had joined from West Bromwich Albion with help from the fund, became the latest player to inherit 31.

"The fans are obviously a massive part of the club," he said, "it's owned by them, and the whole 1931 thing shows the link between the club and fans."

Alan Crockford helped to set up the fund and he is pleased that it remains an ongoing form of supporter activism.

"We all want to do our bit and it's nice to see that we can play a small part in that process," he said. "This is the tenth season and we've paid in £140,000 over 10 years. Our contribution is doing our bit to chip in and it's nice that we've been able to organise ourselves in such a way that it is a tangible product that we can offer and say, 'We did that, we paid for that.' In that sense, it's a nice scheme."

SPARKES

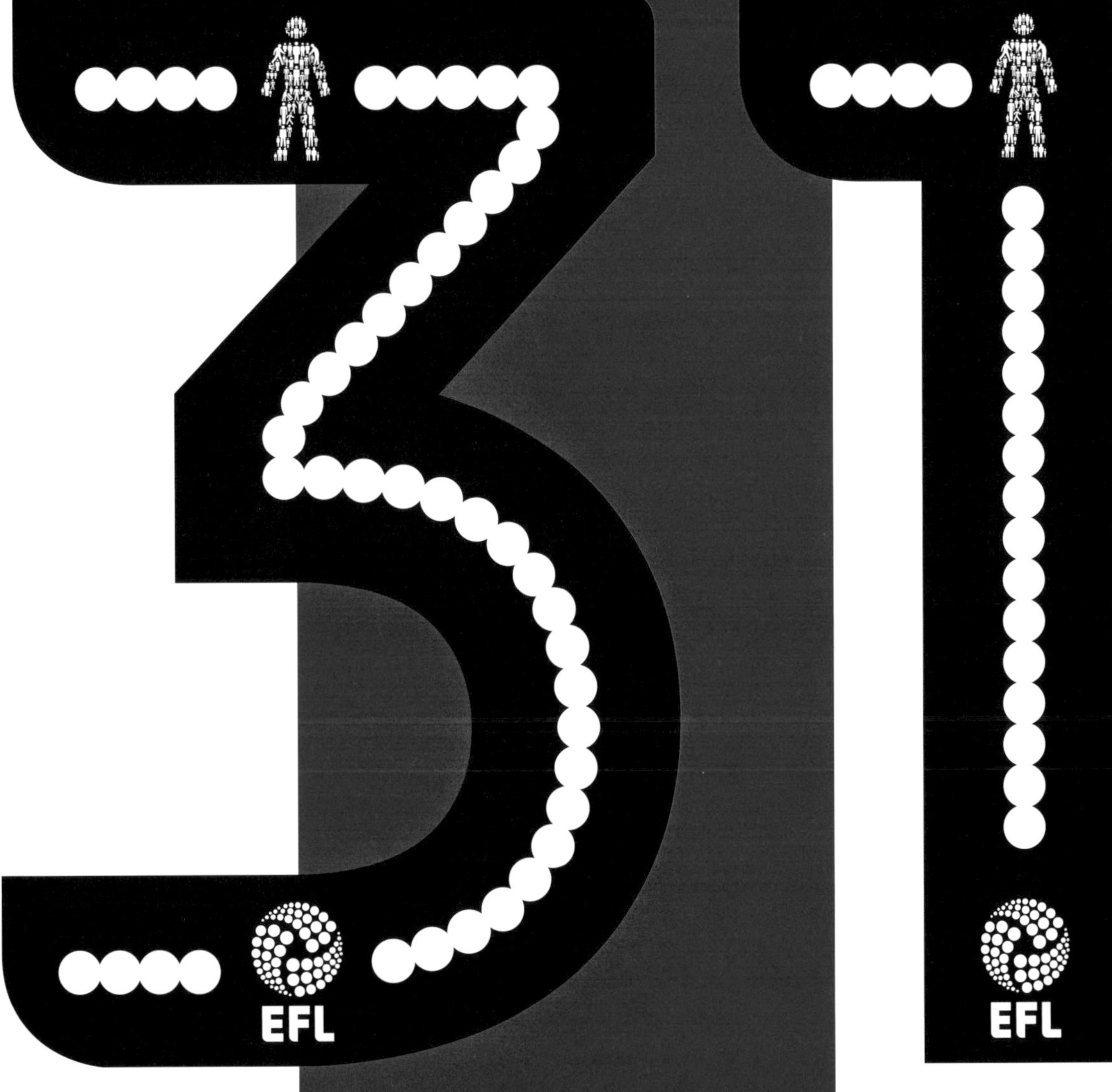

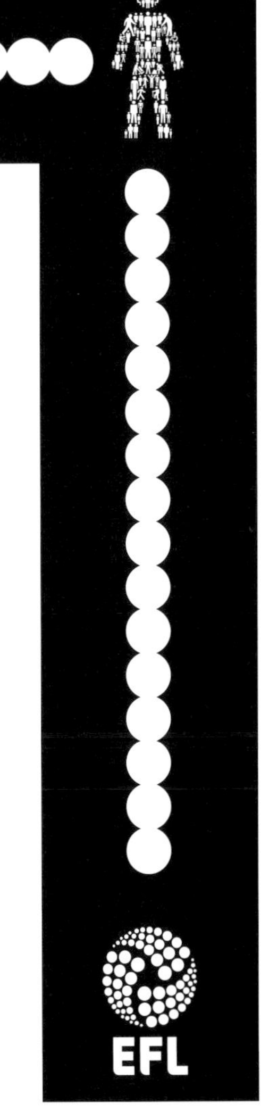

German side St. Pauli has become known for social activism and a left-field approach, and that has carried over to the on-field appearance of the Hamburg club.

Their typeface for 2015-16, coming after they had just avoided relegation to the 2. Bundesliga the previous season, was intended to reflect the ability to improvise and reinvent itself in a sometimes imperfect manner.

The font designed by Nordpol+ was similar to PUMA's 'Gaffer' [p250], with the lettering based on tape, while there were numerous alternative glyphs.

Club
FC St. Pauli

Typeface
FCSP

Year
2016

Design
Nordpol+

Creative Directors
Tim Schierwater &
Sebastian Behrendt

Designer
Jan Volpp

Photography
Witters GmbH

89-..
EFFGG
MNNNN
SSS
YYZZ

While not appearing on the country's shirts – the standard adidas design was used – the Scottish Football Association introduced a new font in 2016.

Created by D8, 'Hampden Display' was intended to communicate a more dynamic and forward-thinking approach both on and off the field.

Using the traditional diamond shape found in the SFA crest as inspiration, D8 created bold, condensed characters with clean, sharp lines and used upward facing crossbars to convey positivity and looking to the future.

Brand
Scottish F.A.

Typeface
Hampden Display

Year
2016

Design
D8

HAMPDEN DISPLAY

ABCDEFGHIJKLM
NOPQRSTUVWXYZ
0123456789,.-£-V-

STEVEN FLETCHER

With Denmark back in the chevrons of Hummel after a period with adidas, the story told within the 2016 home shirt was that of 'Holger Danske' or Ogier The Dane, a hero in Norse mythology.

Hummel wanted to make the typeface feel like runic writing so a Celtic font was distorted. The font for the away shirt was named Messmer, in honour of the brothers who set up Hummel in Hamburg in Germany in 1923.

This latter look was later spread across the Hummel range.

Country
Denmark

Typeface
Celtic Hand (distorted)

Year
2016

Design
Hummel

ABCDEFGHIJKLMNOPQRSTUVWXYZ
ÀÁÂÃÄÆÇÈÉÊËÌÍÎÏÐÑÒÓÕÖØ
ÙÚÛÜÝÞŁŒŠŶŽ 0123456789 « »

Country
Denmark

Typeface
Messmer

Year
2016

Design
Envision

ERIKSEN

10

ERIKSEN

ABCDEFGHIJKLMN
OPQRSTUVWXYZ

1234567890

Country
Bulgaria

Typeface
Apr 1876

Year
2016

Designer
Stefan Chinoff

DELEV
9
10
6
7
8

Dutch side Vitesse Arnhem employed Newminds design studio to create a special font for the club's 125th anniversary in 2017-18.

The club's crest is split 50-50 between yellow and black, and that halved style is subtly employed in the large, angular numbers, with the dotted effect used on the right-hand side.

A subtle shadow gave the numbers depth while the anniversary was marked with the '125 Jaar' tag.

Club
SBV Vitesse

Typeface
125 years Vitesse

Year
2017

Design
Newminds

Designer
Rinse Elsenga

125
JAAR

ABCDEFGHIJK
LMNOPQRS
TUVWXYZẞÄÖÜ
abcdefghijkl
mnopqrstuvw
xyzßäöü
0123456789
!?/,;:@&%

Club
Fortuna Düsseldorf 1895 e.V.

Typeface
Fortuna Sans

Year
2017

Design
Morphoria Design Collective

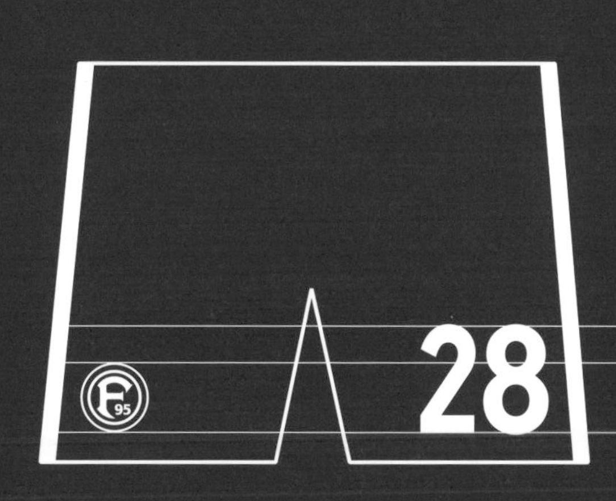

KrjfOwN

Paris Saint-Germain's Nike third kit for the 2017-18 season paid tribute to the city's most iconic landmark, the Eiffel Tower.

The black shirt featured a white stripe down the sleeves, with the pattern imitating the wrought-iron lattice of the famous tower, while the numbers on the back had the same appearance.

Club
Paris Saint-Germain F.C.

Typeface
Custom

Year
2017

Design
Nike

MBAPPÉ
29
CAVANI
9

3

Everton's retail partner, Fanatics, conjured up a retro-style font for the club's Europa League campaign in 2017-18.

The central line stopped before the bottom section of each number so as to allow the club crest to have prominence.

JKLMNOPQRSTUÜVWXYZ.

3456789

ÜVWXYZ.

789

Club
Everton F.C.

Typeface
Everton Euro '17

Year
2017

Design
Fanatics

JKLMNOPQRSTUÜVWXYZ.

3456789

Newminds' brief for the Feyenoord 2017-18 font was to match the rich history of the club. They christened their creation 'Capital F'. Why? Because it was based around the large letter at the centre of the club crest, with the rest of the alphabet based on that.

JØRG

V. PE

V.D. H

Club
Feyenoord

Typeface
Capital F

Year
2017

Design
Newminds

Designer
Rinse Elsenga

NSON RSIE IJDEN

Brand
Premier League

Typeface
Premier League (2017)

Year
2017

Ten years after its last change, the Premier League unveiled a new typeface for numbering and lettering ahead of the 2017-18 season.

Designed by Miles Newlyn, and based on a process which included a survey of more than 1,500 fans and visibility tests with commentator Peter Drury at Watford's Vicarage Road, the new characters were more dynamic and cleaner, with serifs absent.

The five approved colourways were: white with a black outline and black, navy, red, and yellow, all with white outlines.

ABCDEFGHIJKLMNOPQRSTUVWXYZ
ÅÄÆÑÖØÜ#@acdmv.-´`¨ˇ˜

0123456789

0123456789

ABCDEFGHIJKLMNOPQRSTUVWXYZ
ÅÄÆÑÖØÜ#@acdmv.-´`¨ˇ˜

0123456789

0123456789

ABCDEFGHIJKLMNOPQRSTUVWXYZ
ÅÄÆÑÖØÜ#@acdmv.-´`¨ˇ˜

0123456789

0123456789

ABCDEFGHIJKLMNOPQRSTUVWXYZ
ÅÄÆÑÖØÜ#@acdmv.-´`¨ˇ˜

0123456789

0123456789

ABCDEFGHIJKLMNOPQRSTUVWXYZ
ÅÄÆÑÖØÜ#@acdmv.-´`¨ˇ˜

0123456789

0123456789

MESSI
10

Spain's La Liga followed the lead of the Premier League with a rule that mandated teams to use the same font for domestic league games.

However, in August of the 2018-19 season, Real Madrid used their own font in a 2-0 win over Getafe, believing it better emphasised the 'z' in the names of Karim Benzema and Álvaro Odriozola. Ultimately, the uniform league typeface returned.

Spanish teams are still allowed to use fonts of their own choosing for the Copa del Rey and in European competition.

Brand
La Liga

Typeface
Akhand

Year
2017

Design
Indian Type Foundry

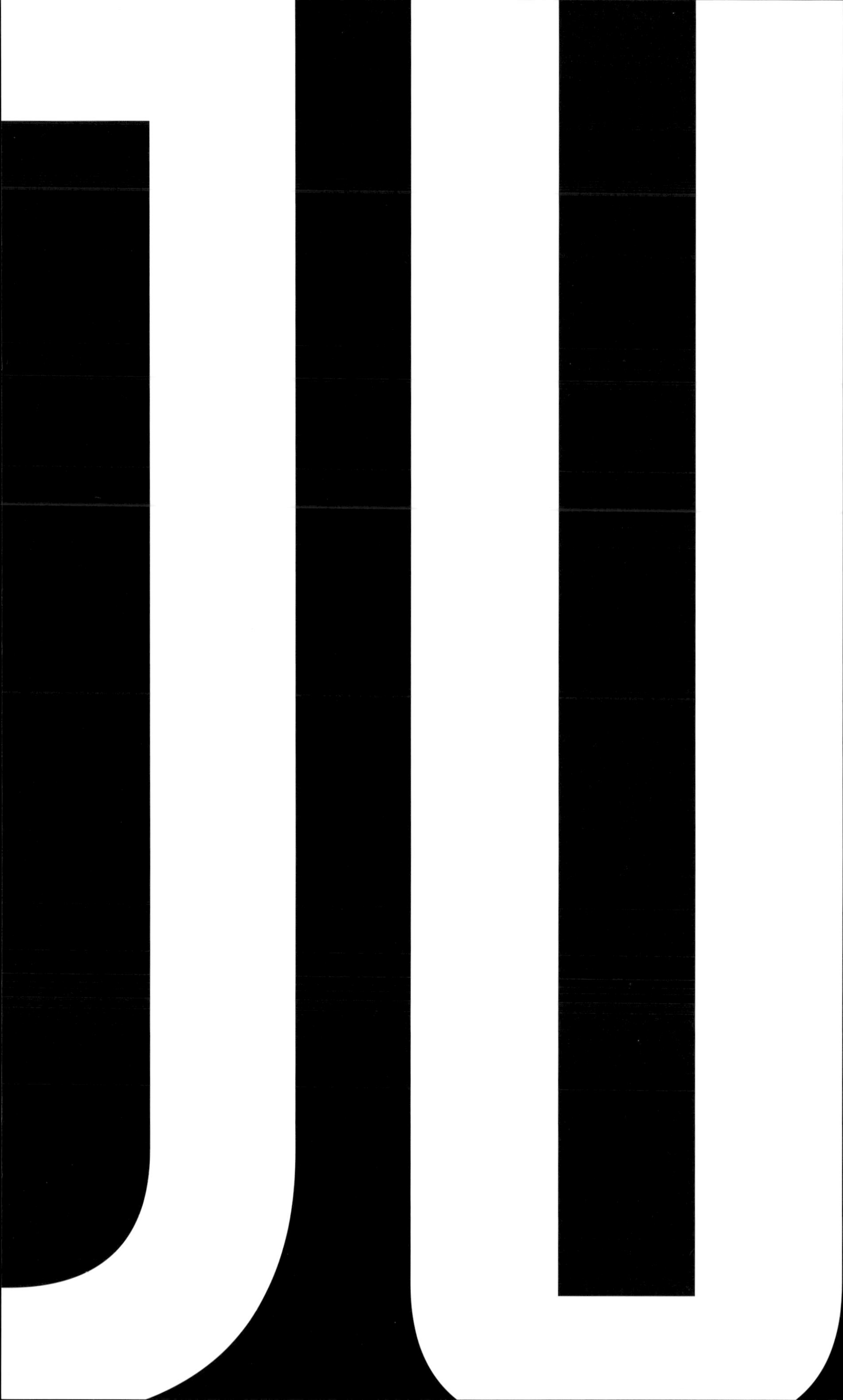

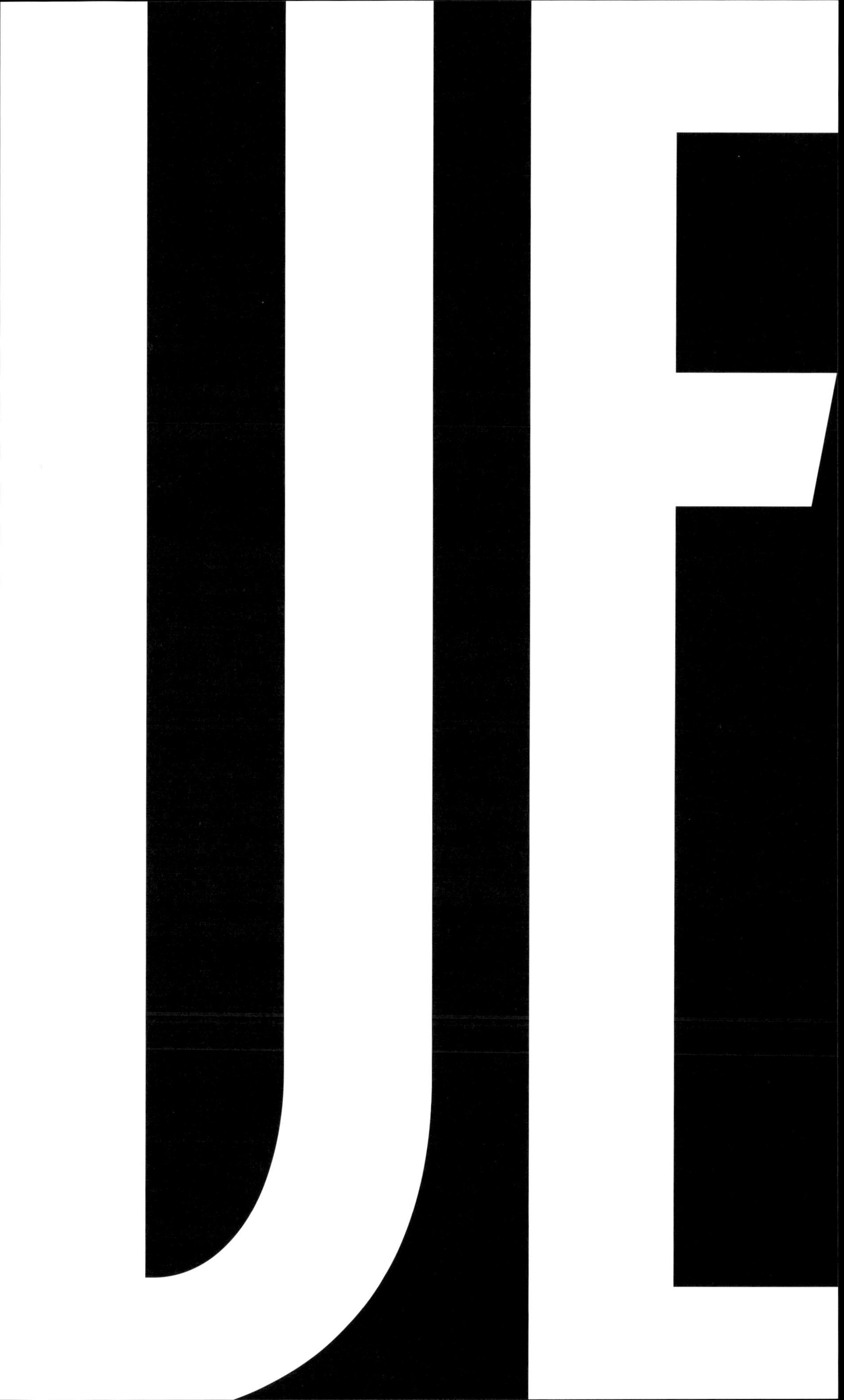

Juventus are one of the most revered clubs in Italy. Established in 1897 and winners of the league title on 37 occasions, the roots of the club's heritage run deep, so creating a new overarching identity was a big challenge for Interband.

The brand consultancy had to transpose the Juventus playing ethos into an idea and attitude that stretched beyond football — appealing to die-hard fans and those whose interest was more casual.

The new typeface — 'Juventus Fans' has a strong rhythm of vertical lines, inspired by the signature black and white stripes of Juventus, while its solid structure gives a strong and sharp appearance.

While primarily considered as a display typeface, other modes and the importance of legibility in small sizes are taken into account with three weights — light, regular and bold — and two super-expressive cuts — bold inline and bold stretched.

Club
Juventus

Typeface
Juventus Fans

Year
2017

Design
Interbrand (Milan)

Global Chief Creative Officer
Andy Payne

Executive Creative Director
Paolo Insinga

Associate Director, Design & Experience
Davide Bignotti

Font Developer
Alessio D'Ellena

LIGHT
ABCDEFGHIJKLMNOPQRSTUVWXYZ
abcdefghijklmnopqrstuvwxyz
0123456789!?

REGULAR
ABCDEFGHIJKLMNOPQRSTUVWXYZ
abcdefghijklmnopqrstuvwxyz
0123456789!?

BOLD
ABCDEFGHIJKLMNOPQRSTUVWXYZ
abcdefghijklmnopqrstuvwxyz
0123456789!?

INLINE
ABCDEFGHIJKLMNOPQRSTUVWXYZ
abcdefghijklmnopqrstuvwxyz
0123456789!?

STRECHED
ABCDEFGHIJKLMNOPQRSTUVWXYZ
0123456789!?

CHIELLINI

3

JUVENTUS

The flag of the Dutch city, Utrecht, is red and white, halved diagonally, and it is reflected in the FC Utrecht crest.

In 2017, Newminds design studio, led by designer Rinse Elsenga, created a font for the club, fittingly called 'Twisting Diagonal'.

Club
FC Utrecht

Typeface
Twisting Diagonal

Year
2017

Design
Newminds

Designer
Rinse Elsenga

ABCDEFG
HIJKLMNOP
QRSTUVWXYZ

12345
67890

F
UTRECHT
C

The summer of 2017 brought a big change for Kelechi Iheanacho as he moved from Manchester City to Leicester City.

There was a notable difference on the back of the Nigerian striker's shirt too. Having worn number 72 at the Etihad Stadium, now he wore 8, while there were two notable additions — dots below the first and last letters of his surname.

The reason for this is that Iheanacho is a member of the Igbo people, an ethnic group that make up a large percentage of the population in southern Nigeria. Iheanacho's hometown is in the state of Imo, where the population is 98 percent Igbo. Jay-Jay Okocha, Nwankwo Kanu and John Obi Mikel are other notable Igbo players.

The Igbo language, which has an estimated 24 million speakers, has vowels featuring underdots, which change the pronunciation of the letter, with the jaw more open and the tongue lower in the mouth.

"In our tradition, the exclamation under the names is very, very important," Iheanacho told *When Saturday Comes*. "For me, it is a way to express where I come from and for people to know I have this tradition and tribe back home. In the village, if they are able to watch the game and see it, they will be proud.

"I saw some other players have their names with accents so I thought maybe it was a possibility. When I was at Manchester City, I didn't have the opportunity. I was a little bit nervous about it coming up from the academy, but coming here I felt I could talk to people about it and see if they could do it."

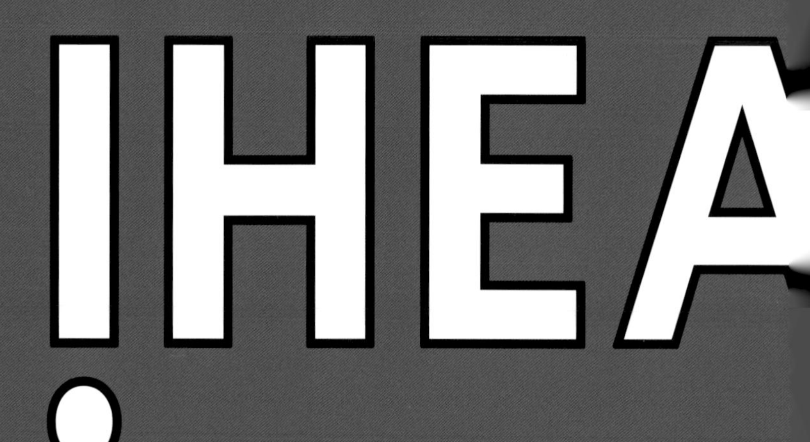

NACHO

Club
Leicester City F.C.

Typeface
Premier League (2017)

Year
2018

Club
'T Knooppunt

Typeface
Cityface

Year
2017

Designer
Floor Wesseling

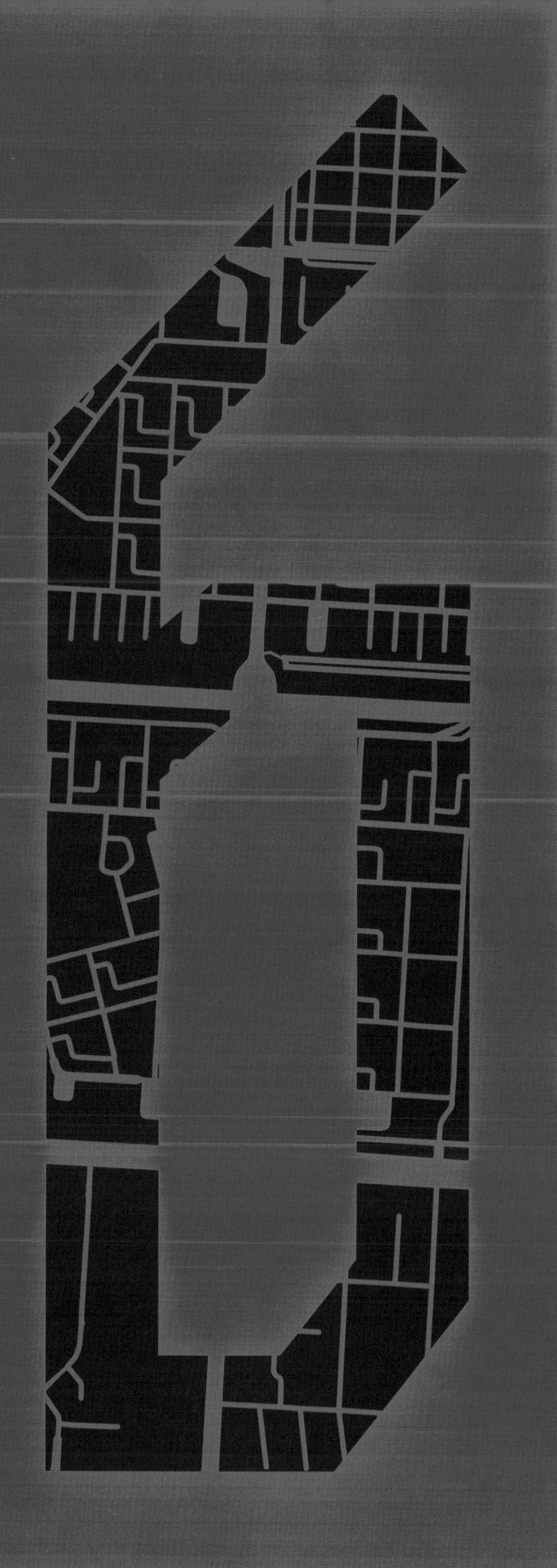

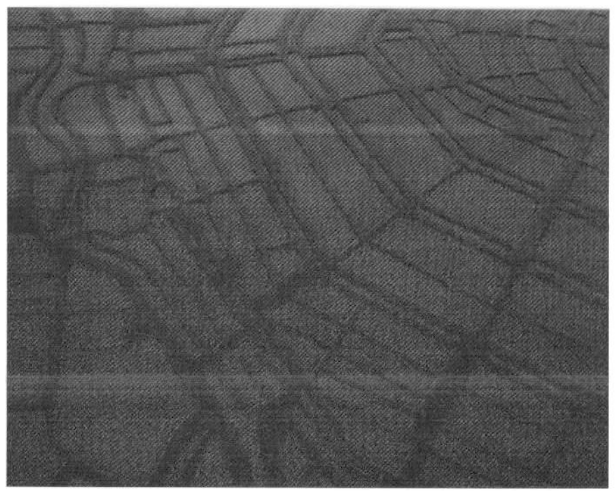

'T Knooppunt is an Amsterdam-based futsal club which recruits high-level, local players and qualified for the UEFA Futal Cup for 2017-18 after winning the D-utch league.

Floor Wesseling was asked to design a kit for the European competition. "My team and I made handmade cut-out flock plots of the city map of Amsterdam in tonal obsidian blue on dark blue shirts," he says.

"As the backs were a mesh fabric, we didn't want to add another flock surface and so we decided to continue the Amsterdam city graphic in the numbers. Each number shows a different part of the map to reflect the idea of continuing the map on the back."

18

34

For its new font for 2017, Manchester United were given another modern reinterpretation of an adidas classic.

Designed by Inigo Turner and Christian Jeffery, the numbers reimagined those used on the 1990-92 away strip [p106].

"This numbering was quite widely used in the period but has a very strong connection to United," Jeffery says.

"It links to iconic moments like the 1991 European Cup Winners' Cup final victory over Barcelona (when a special one-off white kit was worn) and the FA Cup final the year before. It also worked with the kit designs for the seasons very well, bold and solid with integrated ventilation holes to maintain athlete comfort."

GLORY
GLORY
MAN.
UNITED

Club
Manchester United F.C.

Typeface
MUFC 2017

Year
2017

Design
adidas

Designers, adidas
Inigo Turner &
Christian Jeffery

5 cm ABCDEFGHIJKLMNOPQRSTUVWXYZ

25 cm 0123456789

POGBA

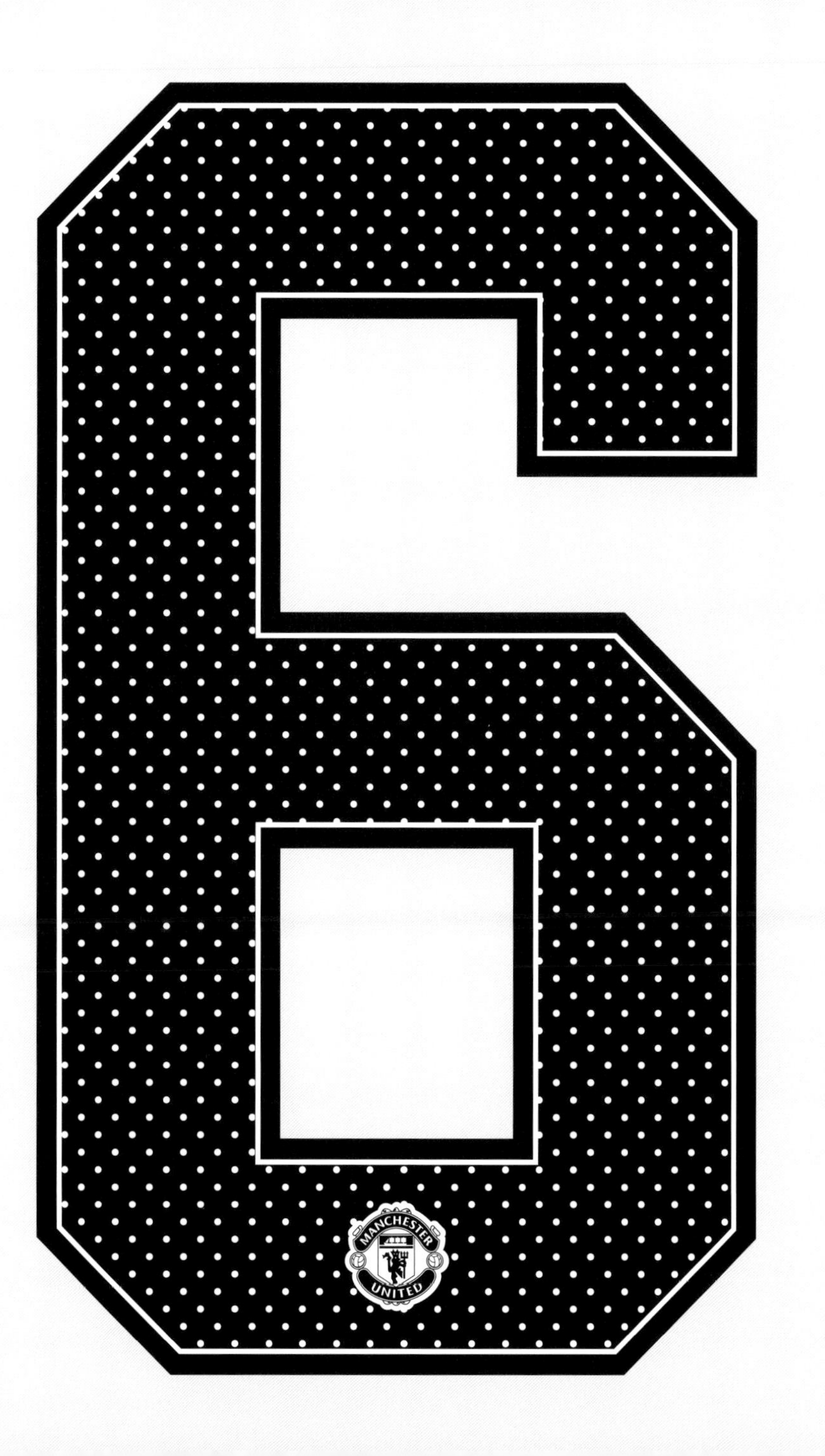

PSV
EST 1913

PSV (Philips Sport Vereniging) was created as the sports team of electrical company Philips in 1913 and has played at Philips Sportpark, later Philips Stadion, since its foundation.

The stadium has undergone many renovations and nowadays it is surrounded by eight striking pillars which provide extra strength. The unique shape of the pillars was the inspiration for PSV's new typeface in 2017, with each character having an asymmetrical cut to represent them.

DE WIJS
ZOET
LUNDQVIST
ARIAS
DE JONG
RIGO
RAMSELAAR

Club
PSV Eindhoven

Typeface
Stadium Pillars

Year
2017

Design
Newminds

Designers
Rinse Elsenga

Club

FC Shakhtar Donetsk

Typeface
Custom

Year
2017

SANNELLA

Club
Calcio Foggia

Typeface
Custom

Year
2017

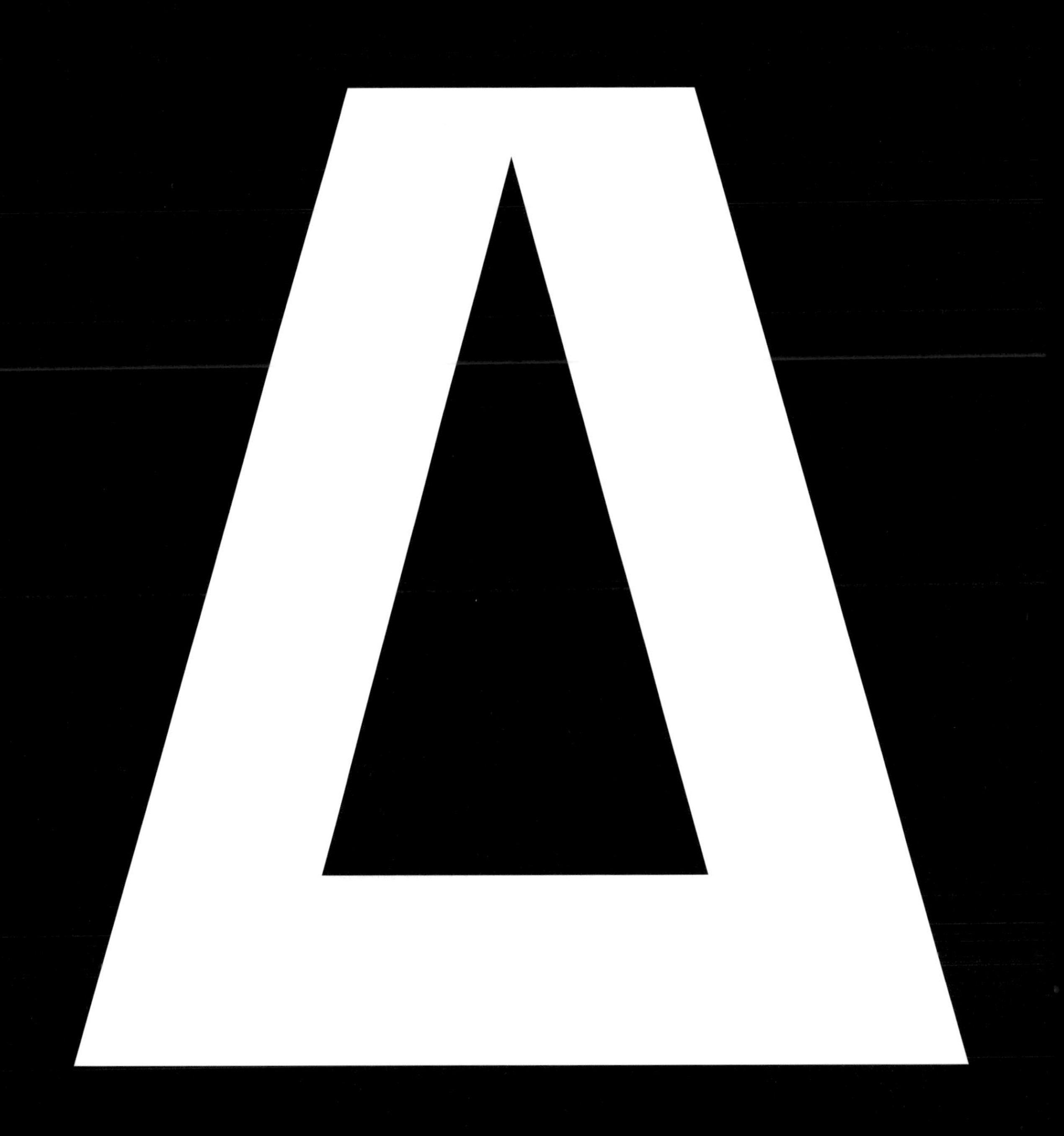

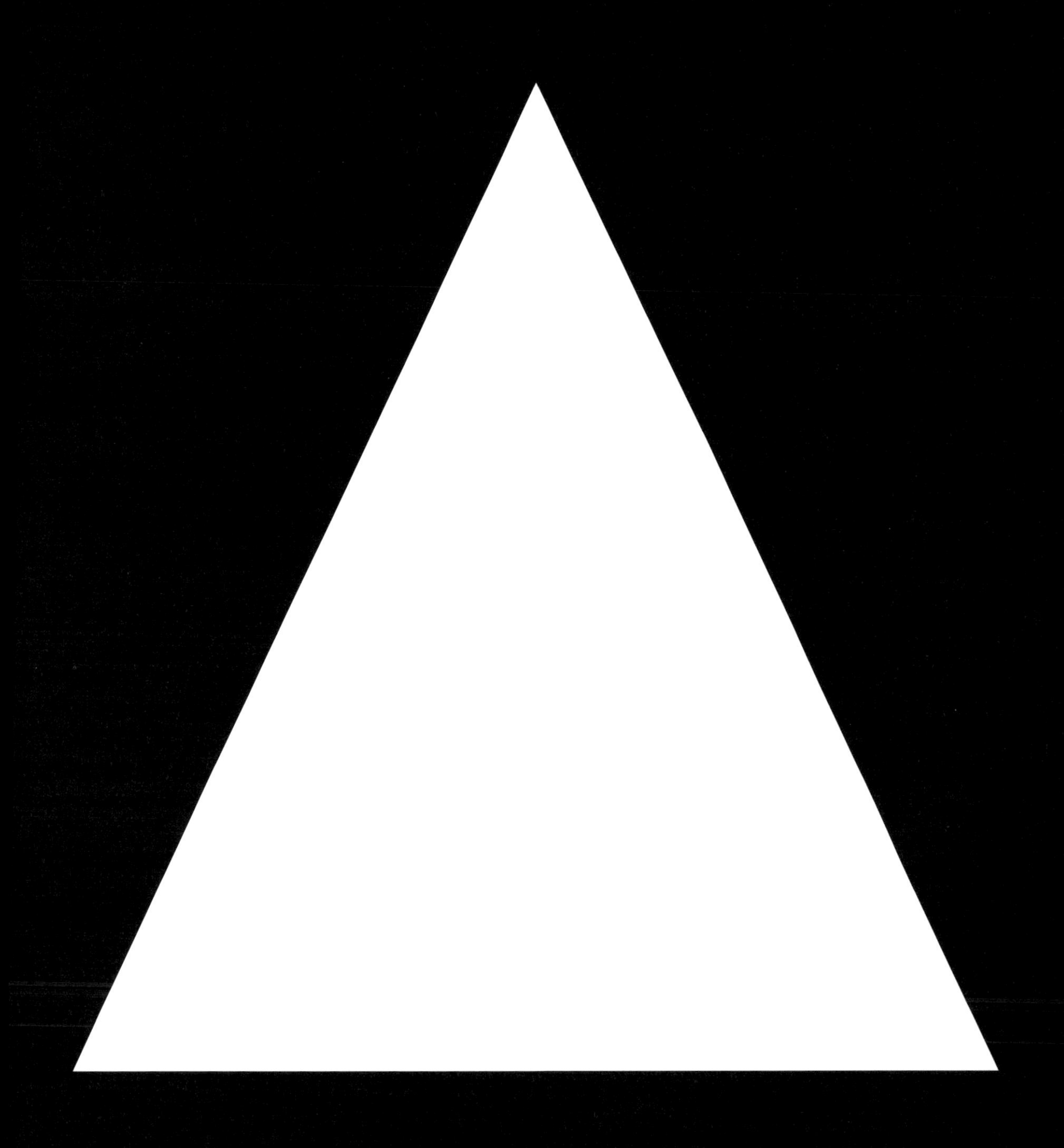

During the 2018 World Cup in Russia, KOSMOS Architects created the Nike Box in Moscow's Gorky Park.

The 4,685-square-metre site included an outdoor football court and visitors were invited to create their own custom jerseys from different kinds of fabrics, a bespoke Nike typeface and additional emblems and logo sets.

Loosely based on Russian Suprematist letterings, the alphabets are designed as distinct units while having individual characters that do not repeat and can be interchanged.

123456
7890

Brand
Nike

Typeface
Gorky

Year
2018

Art Direction, Nike
Wai Lau, Morgan Ruby, Andy Walker & Daniel Whiteneck

Project Management, Nike
Harmen Scheppers & Maryte Klizs

Type design, Dinamo
Johannes Breyer & Fabian Harb

Cyrillic Consulting
Maria Doreuli & Elizaveta Rasskazova

Photography
Nike

ABCDEFGHIJK
LMNOPQR
STUVWXYZ

АБВГДЕЖЗИЙ
КЛМНОПРС
ТУФХЦЧШЩ
ЪЫЬЭЮЯ

PUMA's angular 2018 font had industrial influences, with elongated shapes and recesses at the top and bottom as well as halfway up each side.

The lead designer, Ulrich Planer, acknowledged: "They are definitely not eye-pleasing, but there is a reason behind it."

"Basically, primacy had to be given to the construction of the lightweight PUMA evoKNIT shirt, which included a series of mesh inserts to cool the body, and so the 'cut-outs' meant that the numbers would allow for breathability."

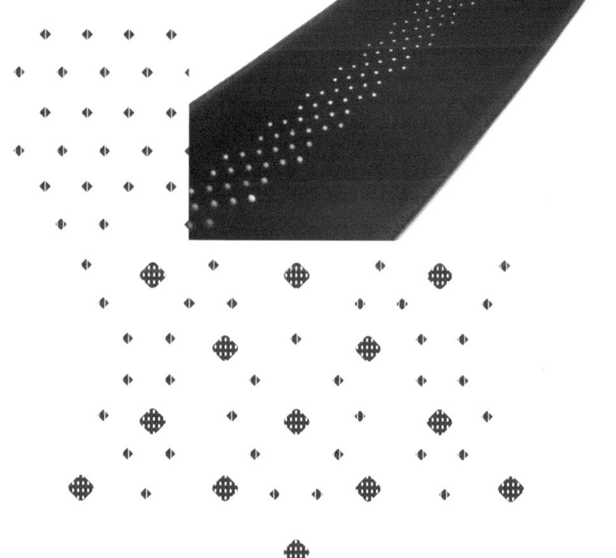

Club & Countries
Names & numbers for all PUMA teams

Typeface
PUMAGANDA

Year
2018

Design
PUMA

Designer, PUMA
Ulrich Planer

ABCDEFGHIJKLMN
OPQRSTUVWXYZ
1234567890

LICHTSTEINER

1234567890

a B C D
e F G H
I J K L
m n o P
Q R S T
U V W X
Y Z

Country
Nigeria

Typeface
Naija

Year
2018

Design
Nike

Designer, Nike
Matthew Wolff

1234567890

A B C D
E F G H
I J K L
M N O P
Q R S T
U V W X
Y Z

Country
France

Typeface
Deco Moderne

Year
2018

Design
Nike

Designer, Nike
Matthew Wolff

KANE

Craig Ward was asked to design t-he custom typeface for England's 2018 W-orld Cup kit and his main aim was to "create something dynamic that hinged on the St George's Cross icon".

He says: "I began by looking at the clarity and geometry of classic English typefaces (Gill, Flaxman, Johnston, etc.) — particularly when condensed, as that was also a requirement.

"I noticed how they lost some of their implied geometry in these instances and decided to create something that didn't buckle like that. Parts of the type actually quote aspects of other fonts to feel a little more familiar — the W in Railway Sans in particular, and the flare of the alternate R is a nod to Gill. I also included a perfectly circular O should they want to use it."

He created the core of the type in 3D software, making a simple grid and drawing single line paths for the letterforms, and then adding a cross as a sweep around the path. This went on to inform the line aspect and the twists in the letters.

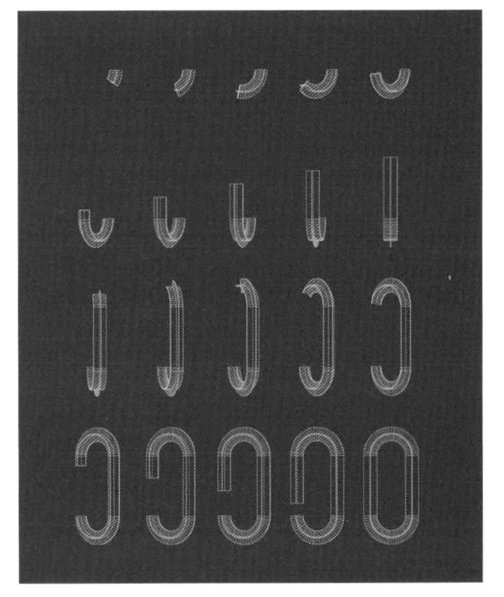

Country
England

Typeface
ENT × Ward

Year
2018

Design
Nike

Art Director, Nike
Kenny McIver

Designer
Craig Ward

ABCDEFGHIJKLMN
OPQRSTUVWXYZ

012345
6789

PICKFORD
MAGUIRE
STONES
WALKER
TRIPPIER
YOUNG
HENDERSON
LINGARD
ALLI
STERLING
KANE

For the 2018 World Cup in Russia, adidas adopted the design direction "from authenticity to progression", with the competing countries given modernised versions of classic jersey styles.

To complement those, the German company wanted an iconic new font. Senior designer Christian Jeffery says that adidas looked to the past, both to the usage of bold numbers and the various lined styles, combining both characteristics to have a bold look with just one line in the centre.

The straight-line lettering was inspired by the Cyrillic alphabet and Soviet aesthetic.

"Next to that," Jeffery says, "we wanted to keep it as reduced and simple as possible by not changing too much from the strong block look. The hard angles linked also very nicely to the panel shape of the Telstar ball.

"The result was a very iconic font which was created to catch attention. This was a bold font, which will always be associated with this tournament, like many other adidas designs from the past – which are associated with their respective tournaments."

Club & Countries
Names & numbers for all adidas teams

Typeface
adidas WC 2018

Year
2018

Design
adidas

Senior Designer, adidas
Christian Jeffery

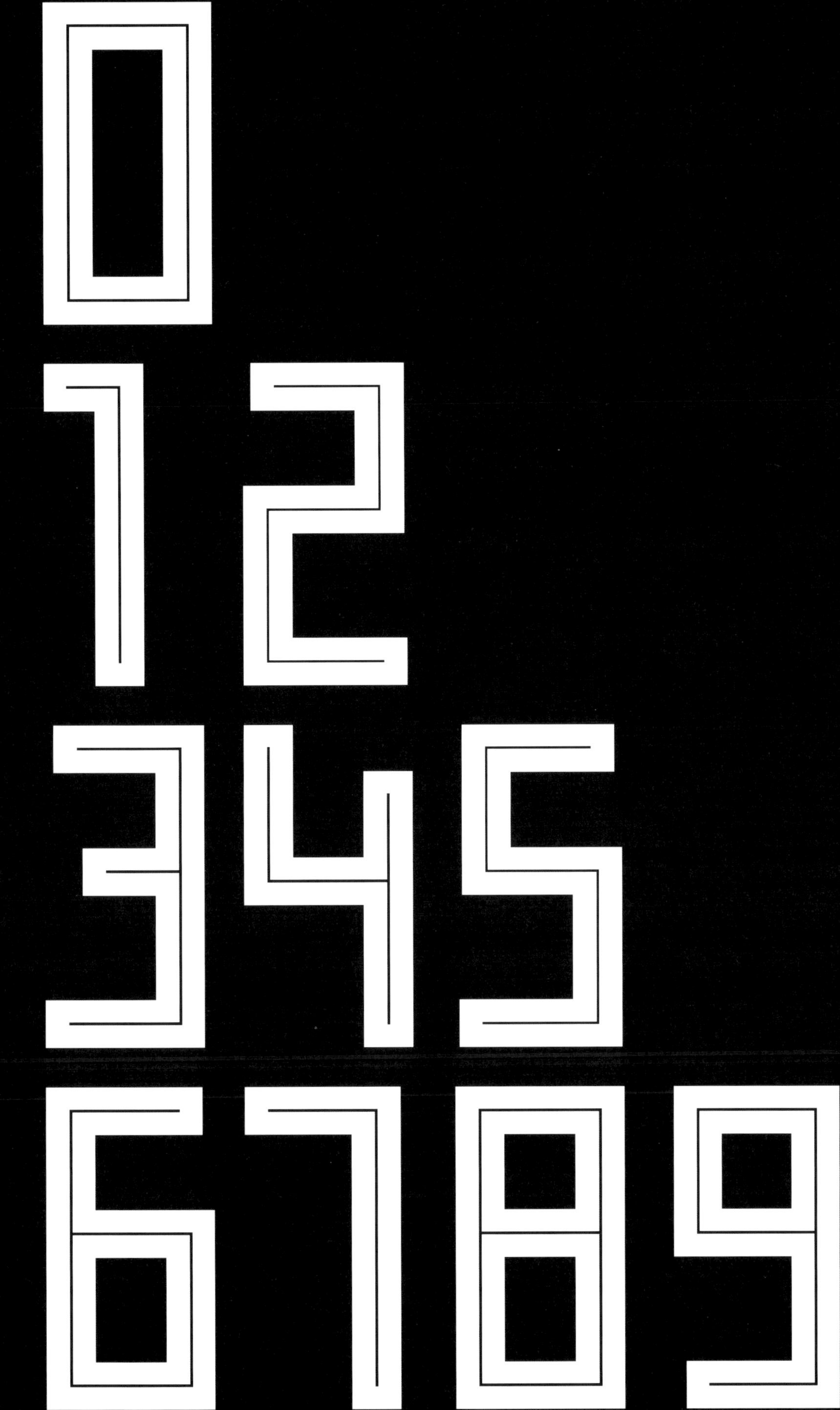
0
12
345
6789

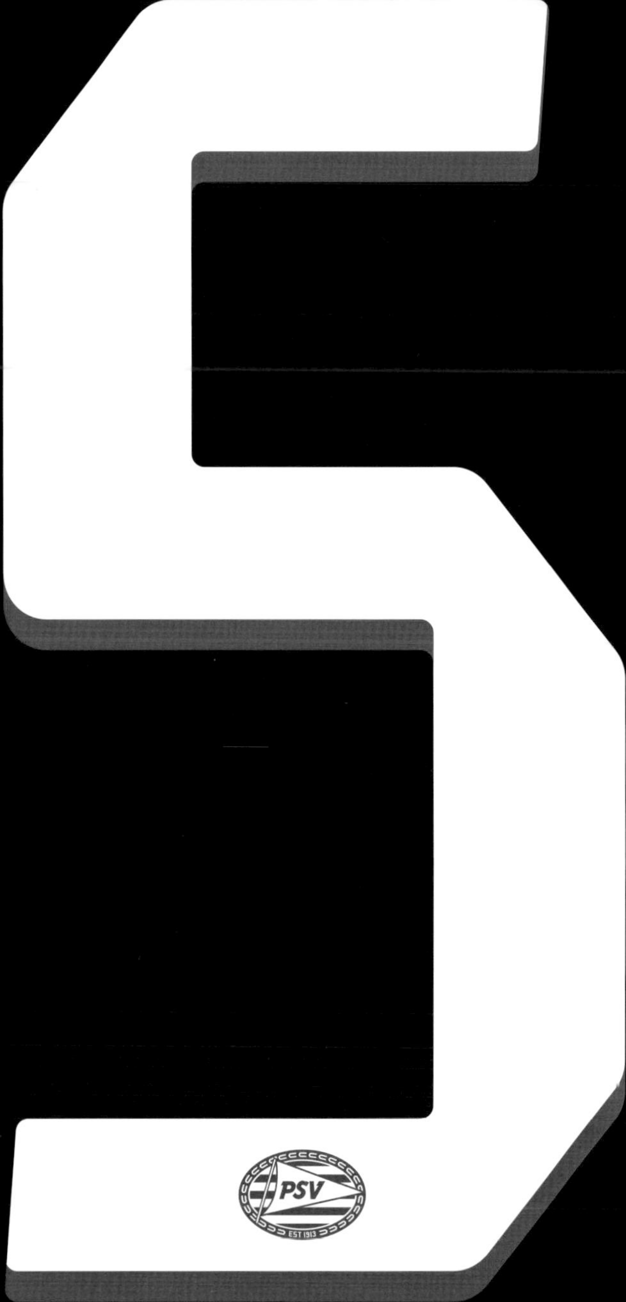
PSV
EST 1913

PSV
PSV

In pre-season, before the 2018-19 campaign, Arsenal competed in the International Champions Cup in Singapore and the Gunners sported a special-edition typeface.

Against Atlético Madrid, the home kit was worn, with the new mint-green third kit used against Paris Saint-Germain. Both featured numbering designed by sneaker artist and streetwear designer Mark Ong.

The three-dimensional designs were typical of the Singaporean artist's style and included several local landmarks, including Changi Airport's control tower, the Singapore Flyer, Marina Bay Sands and Merlion Park.

Club
Arsenal F.C.

Typeface
SBTG × PUMA

Year
2018

Design
SBTG

Designer
Mark Ong

AUBAMEYANG

After promotion to the Premier League in 2018, Wolverhampton Wanderers commissioned SomeOne to come up with a new distinctive design personality for the club.

As founder members of the Football League in 1888, the brief required an acknowledgement of past glories and the exciting present and future. SomeOne took inspiration from the iconic crest and the city's industrial heritage to design a typeface using the triangular forms of the wolf's eyes.

While some clubs use bespoke fonts in cup competitions, Wolves opted for the standard Premier League typeface in 2018-19, but this unique one appeared on Europa League shirts in 2019 as the club made a return to European football for the first time since 1980-81.

Club
Wolverhampton Wanderers F.C.

Typeface
Wolves Display

Year
2018

Design
SomeOne

Designers
Ian Dawson, Rich Rhodes, Gary Holt & Tim Green

ABCDEFGHI
JKLMNOPQR
STUVWXYZ
0123456789
#/\!?&£()[]“
ÁÂÄÉÍÓÚÜÑ¿¡
ÃÀÇÉÊÍÓÔÕÚ

AABBCCDDEEFF
GGHHIIJJKKLL
MMNNOOPPQQ
RRSSTTUUVV
WWXXYYZZ
001122334455
66778899

NEYMAR JR
10

MBAPPÉ
7

Designer Alexis Taïeb, aka TYRSA, created an exclusive typeface to celebrate the 2018 collaboration between Air Jordan and Paris Saint-Germain.

This was achieved by scanning a classic basketball typeface and distorting it manually. As he says, "No Photoshop was used here – only my random gesture while holding and moving my piece of paper on the scanner window!"

Thin lines, common in football fonts, were added to the centre of each digit. Each letter and figure had two different options, to allow for unique choices and the avoidance of duplication.

Club
Paris Saint-Germain F.C.

Typeface
Custom

Year
2018

Designer
Alexis Taïeb (TYRSA)

Liverpool's previous typeface from 2010-18 [p234] certainly didn't owe anybody anything and a new custom font was introduced for the 2018-19 season.

The main point of reference was the lettering font used on the main stadium signage at the club's Anfield home, as well as that used on street signs throughout the city of Liverpool.

Depth was added to the numbering with the incorporation of a bold drop shadow seen in the seating within the stadium itself. The base for the custom font was Helvetica Neue Bold Condensed.

Club
Liverpool F.C.

Typeface
Croft

Year
2018

Design
Avery

VIRGIL

4

MANÉ

KARIUS

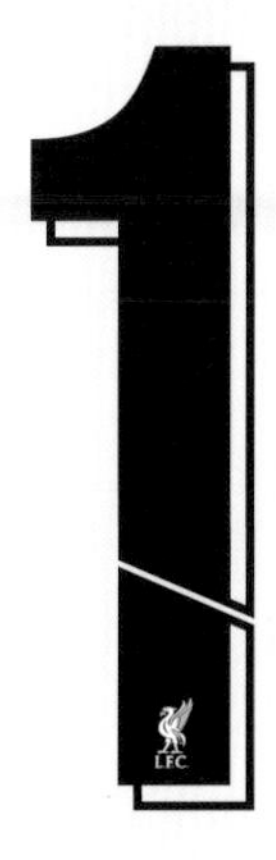

MIGNOLET

In 2018, when UEFA sought to rebrand the Champions League, DesignStudio collaborated with type designers Fontsmith to create a new weight of the brand's existing typeface, 'Champions'.

The designers felt that the new light weight reflected the skill and precision required at the top level, while centred layouts and wide tracking expressed the scale and grandeur of European club football's signature competition.

Brand
UEFA Champions League

Typeface
Champions

Year
2018

Design
DesignStudio

Type Design
Fontsmith

CHAMPIONS LIGHT

ABCDEFGHIJKLMNOPQRSTUVWXYZ
abcdefghijklmnopqrstuvwxyz
0123456789!@#€£&%*(),."

CHAMPIONS REGULAR

ABCDEFGHIJKLMNOPQRSTUVWXYZ
abcdefghijklmnopqrstuvwxyz
0123456789!@#€£&%*(),."

CHAMPIONS BOLD

ABCDEFGHIJKLMNOPQRSTUVWXYZ
abcdefghijklmnopqrstuvwxyz
0123456789!@#€£&%*(),."

CHAMPIONS EXTRA BOLD

ABCDEFGHIJKLMNOPQRSTUVWXYZ
abcdefghijklmnopqrstuvwxyz
0123456789!@#€£&%*(),."

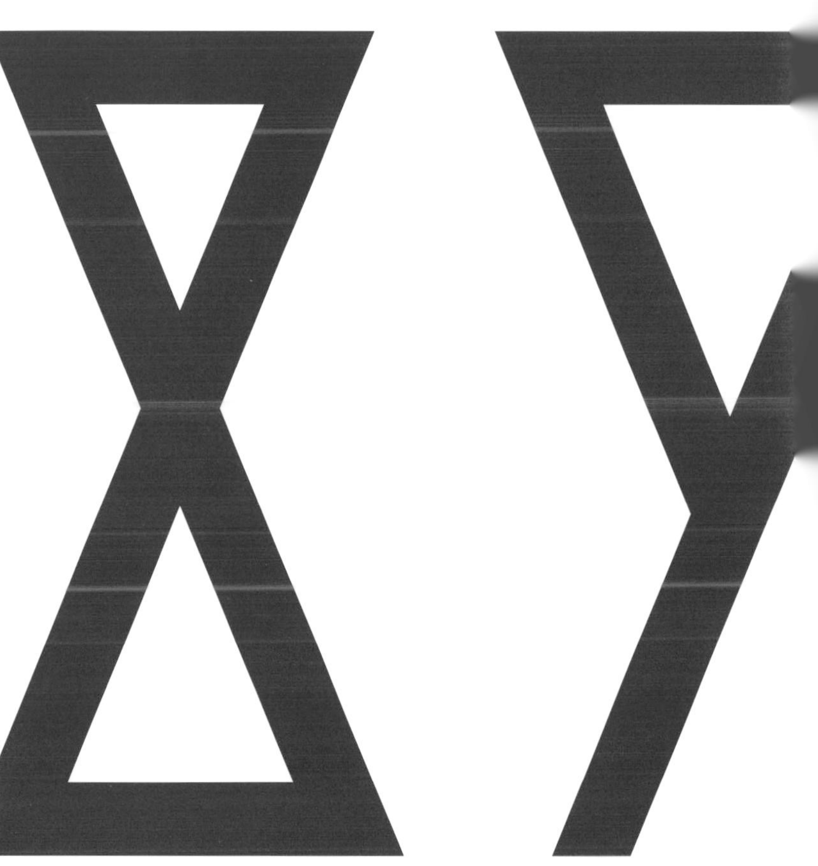

While Floor Wesseling is a top designer, that doesn't mean that he limits himself to the top teams.

He has played for Zeeburgia for about 20 years and naturally he assumed the role of kit manager too, designing bespoke kits since 2007, with the home and away alternating in two-year cycles.

"We've played in 'poker shirts', a variety of 'formation shirts', Amsterdam shirts and currently in a 'directional' home shirt with arrows on the sleeves," he says. "Why? Because we can. "

As the club's "seventh team", the typeface revolves around the shape of the number 7. "Legibility is a bitch sometimes but hey, who cares, we play in the fifth division in the Dutch Saturday league!" he laughs.

Club
Zeeburgia Zaterdag 7

Typeface
Magnificent 7

Year
2018

Design
Wesseling

Designer
Floor Wesseling

On April 17, 2018, for the Serie A game with Cagliari, Inter Milan celebrated what it billed as #InterSocialNight and, to mark the occasion, the club's dressing room was set up with players' shirts bearing their Instagram (or Intergram?) handles.

This was only a promotion though and, for the game itself, surnames were worn over the numbers, as per league rules.

Club
Inter Milan

Typeface
Custom (distorted)

Year
2018

@DSANTON21
21
Driver
ONTI
21

Club
Paris Saint-Germain F.C.

Typeface
Custom

Year
2018

Design
Nike

As seen in many of the early offerings from the 1960s and 1970s, American sports influenced football design and the wheel came full-circle with the collaboration between Paris Saint-Germain and Air Jordan in 2018.

While the Nike swoosh continued to feature on PSG's domestic kits, a new set of strips and ancillary leisurewear was introduced for the Champions League, featuring the Jumpman logo.

Fittingly, the lettering on the back was more than similar to that of the Chicago Bulls, for whom Michael Jordan played from 1984-98.

When PSG played Manchester United in the 2018-19 Champions League, Mason Greenwood was a late call-up to the United squad, so late that a proper kit hadn't been prepared for him. The Red Devils availed of PSG's numbering and lettering for a quickly made-up shirt – luckily, the English club's typography was quite similar [p366].

NEYMAR JR

0123456789

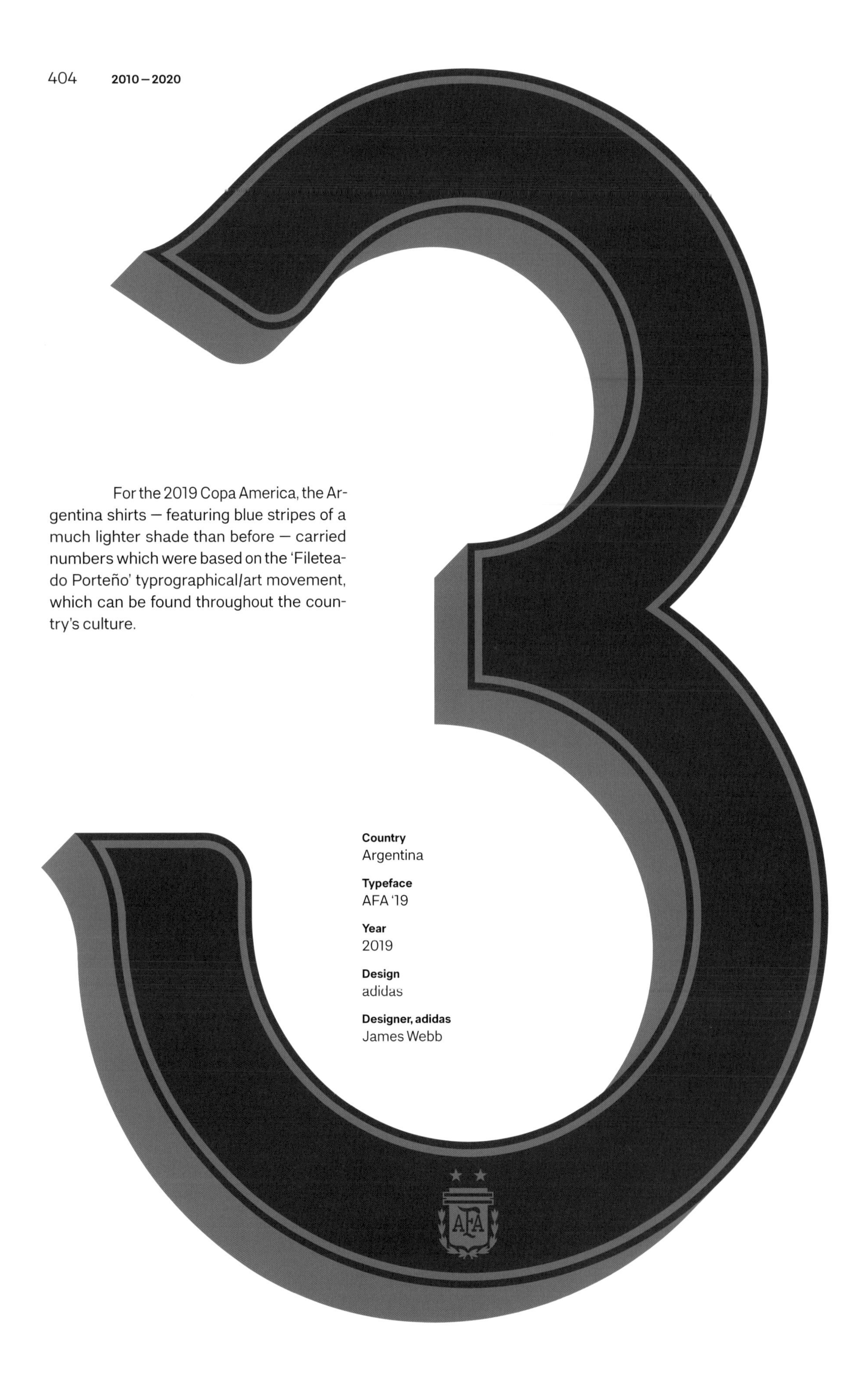

For the 2019 Copa America, the Argentina shirts — featuring blue stripes of a much lighter shade than before — carried numbers which were based on the 'Fileteado Porteño' typrographical/art movement, which can be found throughout the country's culture.

Country
Argentina

Typeface
AFA '19

Year
2019

Design
adidas

Designer, adidas
James Webb

The 'sombrero vueltiao', or 'turned hat', is a traditional Colombian symbol. It is made from caña fleche, a type of cane that grows in the region, and is the basis for the 2019 Colombia shirt and numbering.

The jersey focuses on a lenticular representation of the traditional patterns that adorn the hats as well as the skirts of cumbia dancers, with the letters and numbers meant to compliment the graphic with a more rounded approach. Elements of the graphic can be found within the number's cut-out, linking the two together.

Country
Columbia

Typeface
FCF '19

Year
2019

Design
adidas

Designer, adidas
James Webb

R. JIMENEZ

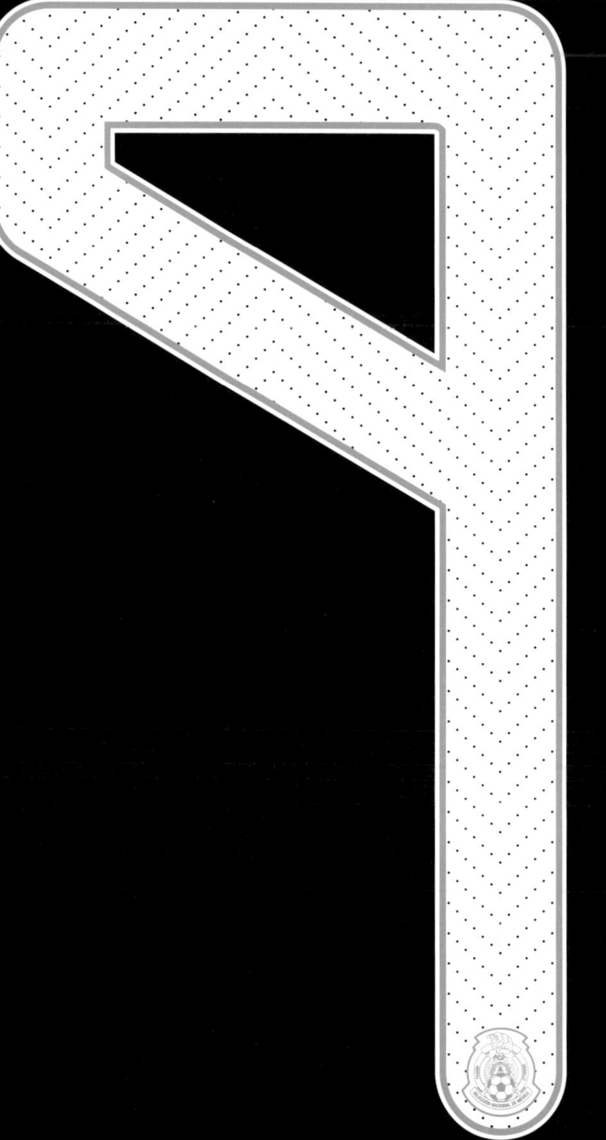

01234
56789

ABCDEFGHIJKLMNOPQRSTUVWXYZ
ÁÉÍÑÓÚÜ -/.

ABCDEF

NOPQRS

12345

Club
A.C. Milan

Typeface
Milan Pulse Inline

Year
2019

Design
DixonBaxi

Type Design
Elliott Amblard

HIJKLM

UVWXYZ

67890

BRIGHT

Brand
Women's FA

Typeface
FAW

Year
2019

Design
Nomad

01234
56789

ABCDEFGHIJKLMN
OPQRSTUVWXYZ

ABCDEFGHIJ
KLMNOPQRS
TUVWXYZ

1234567890

Designers must always take into account where letters and numbers will be placed — a brilliantly-executed font may not be fully appreciated, simply because of the noise around it.

To that end, because PUMA's 2019 shirts are graphic-driven, with a number of flourishes, the accompanying numbers are simple and neutral, so as not to distract.

Club & Countries
Names & numbers for all PUMA teams

Typeface
PUMA Futbol

Year
2019

Design
PUMA

Designers, PUMA
Ulrich Planer & Felix Kraus

To mark the 60th anniversary of the UEFA European Championship, the 2020 competition will be held across 12 countries. Uniting art and football, each design is inspired by the similarities that exist between these territories. Taking inspiration from the shapes of fonts used on European passports and number plates, each letter and number is filled with artwork on a matte background and framed by a glossy outline. Japan is the noticeable exception as they obviously won't feature in the competition.

Countries
Spain, Sweden, Belgium & Japan

Typeface
adidas Euro 2020

Year
2019

Design
adidas

Designer, adidas
James Webb

What better way to finish than with the new MLS font, designed by the book's designer, Rick Banks?

Commissioned by the league to mark its 25th season, the typeface is symbolic of the progressive nature of the MLS. Inspired by the 'Penrose triangle', it makes for a bold and dynamic look, with the 'swooshing' optical effect embodying the movement and energy of a football game. The tri-line motif also references the three stars of the league logo.

Given the vast array of countries represented in the MLS, it was important to allow for long names and diacritics and the font does this, as well as coming in three weights. The versatility is shown in how MLS Streets is displayed on playing kit, while the other weights can be used on banners around stadia, online and for social media.

Brand
MLS

Typeface
MLS Pitch,
MLS Streets &
MLS Stands

Year
2020

Design
Face37

Foundry
F37 Foundry

!#$$%&'()*+,-.//0123456789:;<≡=>

?@ABCDEFGHIJKLMNOPQRSTUVW

XYZ[\]_D{|}~¡£¦§©¬®°¶·¿ÀÁÂÃÄÅ

ÆÇÈÉÊËÌÍÎÏÐÑÒÓÔÕÖ×ØØÙÚÛÜÝÞ

÷ŸĀĂĄĆĊČĎĐĒĖĘĚĞĠĢĦĪĮİĶĹĻĽŁŃ

ŅŇŊŌŐŒŔŖŘŚŞŠŢŤŦŪŮŰŲŴŶŹŻŽ

ȘȚẀẂẄỲ–—‘’‚“”„†‡…‰/€™−∫≠

MLS STREETS CONDENSED
FOR SUPER LONG NAMES

MLS PITCH

ABCDEFGHIJKL
MNOPQRSTUVWXYZ
0123456789

MLS STREETS

ABCDEFGHIJKL
MNOPQRSTUVWXYZ
0123456789

MLS STANDS

ABCDEFGHIJKL
MNOPQRSTUVWXYZ
0123456789

BLES
DEFEND THE FORTRESS
NANI
17
12345

67890

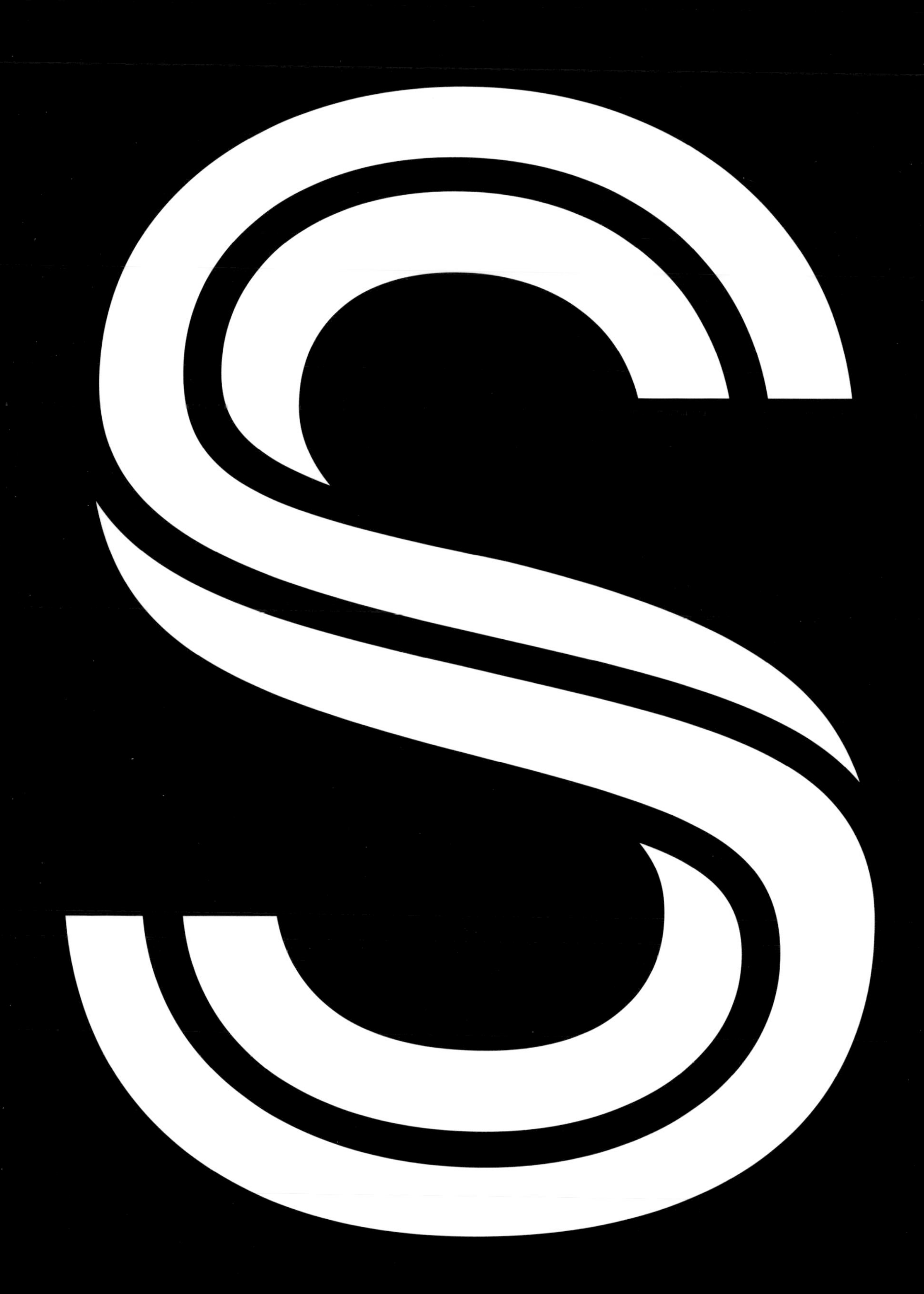

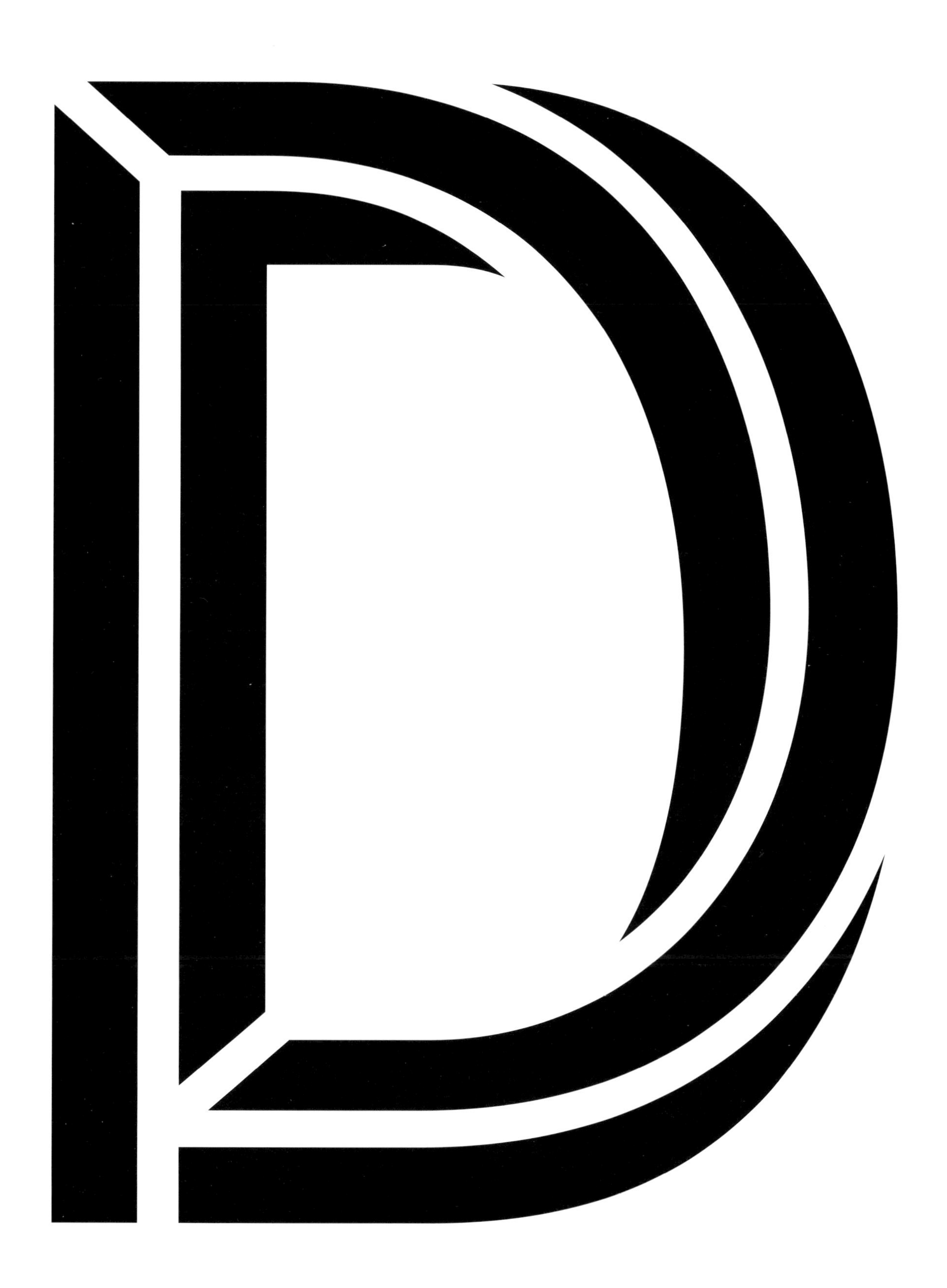

Thank you to everyone who helped make this book happen:

Alejandro Ortega Serrano
Alessio D'Ellena
Alexander Banks
Andrea Dal Canton
Andy Walker
Anna Gnudi
Anthony Barnett
Ben Earnshaw
Campbell Butler
Caterina Piras
Chris Jennions
Christoph Koeberlin
Corinne Myers
David Bruce
Dave Morrison (nasljerseys.com)
Emma Oliver
Francesca Cianfarini
Heidi Burgett
Ian Cherry
Ian Croft
James Webb
Joe Dick
Jonathan Dykes
Jonathan Finlay
Julia McAulay
Jürgen Rank
Kasper Hald Morsø
Kevin Coatman
Kenny McIver
Leo Philip
Lesley Ramshaw
Luke Prowse
Mhairi McLaughlin
Nick Holt
Olivier Antonio Bara Negro
Olivier Vinet
Paul Nagel (unitedkits.com)
Paul Jolleys
Rob Baker
Rob Urbani
Robert Holmkvist
Sam Smith
Tam Handley
Thibault Chevillard
Tim Whitehead
Terry Stephens
Tom Lippiett
Turner Inigo
Ulrich Planner